THE JAYHAWK

®

THE JAYHAWK

THE STORY OF THE
UNIVERSITY OF KANSAS'S
BELOVED MASCOT

REBECCA OZIER SCHULTE

University Press of Kansas

Published by the University Press of Kansas (Lawrence, Kansas 66045), which was organized by the Kansas Board of Regents and is operated and funded by Emporia State University, Fort Hays State University, Kansas State University, Pittsburg State University, the University of Kansas, and Wichita State University.

Photographs on the following pages taken by Elizabeth Schulte Esparza: 13, 39 (*bottom left* and *bottom right*), 58 (*top*), 109 (*middle, bottom left,* and *bottom right*), 124 (*top right* and *bottom*), 122, 129 (*top right* and *bottom*), 131 (*top left* and *top right*), 137 (*top* and *bottom*), 139, 152 (*top* and *bottom*), 153, 155 (*top*).

Library of Congress Cataloging-in-Publication Data

Names: Schulte, Rebecca Ozier, author.
Title: The Jayhawk : the story of the University of Kansas's beloved mascot
  / Rebecca Ozier Schulte.
Description: Lawrence, Kansas : University Press of Kansas, 2023. |
  Includes index.
Identifiers: LCCN 2022055990
  ISBN 9780700635399 (cloth : alk. paper)
Subjects: LCSH: University of Kansas—Sports—History. | Sports team
  mascots—Kansas—History.
Classification: LCC GV691.U542 S35 2023 | DDC 796.04/3—dc23/eng/20230306
LC record available at https://lccn.loc.gov/2022055990.

British Library Cataloguing-in-Publication Data is available.

Printed in China

10 9 8 7 6 5 4 3 2 1

The paper used in this publication is acid free and meets the minimum requirements of the American National Standard for Permanence of Paper for Printed Library Materials Z39.48-1992.

To my husband, Dan, my daughters Emily and Lizzie,
my grandchildren Dominic, Harper, Evie, Taylor, and Landon,
and my parents, Hugh and Helen Ozier

CONTENTS

FOREWORD, CHANCELLOR
DOUGLAS A. GIROD   IX

ACKNOWLEDGMENTS   XI

1 ORIGIN OF THE JAYHAWK AND THE
  ROCK CHALK YELL   1

2 THE EVOLUTION OF THE JAYHAWK   15

3 THE JAYHAWK AS MASCOT   43

4 JAYHAWKS IN PRINT   63

5 JAYHAWKS AND STUDENT LIFE   91

6 JAYHAWKS IN ADVERTISING   123

7 JAYHAWKS FOR SALE: MEMORABILIA,
  COLLECTIBLES, SOUVENIRS,
  MERCHANDISE   135

8 JAYHAWKS NEAR AND FAR   141

9 JAYHAWKS INTO THE TWENTY-FIRST
  CENTURY   151

INDEX   159

FOREWORD

From Lawrence to Liberal, from the West Coast to the Eastern seaboard, from North America to Asia, few mascots are more recognizable than the University of Kansas's Jayhawk. The yellow-beaked bird has been KU's official mascot since *Daily Kansan* cartoonist Hank Maloy drew the first official Jayhawk in 1912. For students, alumni, and fans, the Jayhawk is a symbol of tradition, excellence, and community.

In this delightful book, Becky Schulte introduces us to the history of the Jayhawk. In students' scrapbooks, in KU yearbooks, and university publications, Schulte guides us along the Jayhawk's journey from the leggy 1912 bird to the fictional fowl we use today. She tells the story of how Big Jay and Baby Jay came to be, including the hair-raising "kidnapping" of the Baby Jay costume in 1978. (Spoiler alert: we got it back.)

The most wonderful feature of the book is the abundance of photographs. Our Jayhawk appears on nearly every page—in cartoons, banners, signs, advertisements, memorabilia, merchandise, on the sides of World War II planes, and even in the Space Shuttle!

The Jayhawk is as educational as it is entertaining, and it will enthrall everyone who cherishes our mascot. Rock Chalk!

Chancellor Douglas A. Girod, University of Kansas

ACKNOWLEDGMENTS

There are many people who took an interest in this project and helped me to track down elusive Jayhawks. I could not have written this book without their assistance and enthusiasm.

Rebecca Smith, who first introduced to me the idea of doing research on the Jayhawk many years ago; the early University Archives staff, John Nugent, Ned Kehde, and Barry Bunch, who collected, organized, and described all that Jayhawk information and without whom I could not have even started this project; Mallory Harrell who combed through boxes and boxes of KU materials to find all those amazing Jayhawks; Kathy Lafferty and Sarah Chapman, who scanned most of the images; my beautiful, talented daughter Lizzie, my official Jayhawk photographer, who was very patient as I said go here, go there, take that photo; Letha Johnson, for her support as my technical guru; Meredith Phares, who helped to obtain materials; Jennifer Sanner, David Johnston, and Susan Younger at the KU Alumni Association, without whose help the book would have been much thinner on the facts; my boss, Beth Whittaker, who has encouraged me all along the way; Tim Gaddie, manager of the unions, who opened up his treasure trove of Jayhawks to me and Britany Johnson, who found the images I needed; Professor Marc Greenberg; Lisa Kring, Jennifer Baker, and Julia Gillman from the Memorial Union; Cris Bandle, the Owens Flower Shop office manager; J. F. Devlin, who designed and provided the HawkHelp Jayhawk; astronaut Steven Hawley; Justin Hill and Mike Cordoba, from the Lawrence Box Company; Clyde Toland, for his knowledge of the life of General Frederick Funston; Lisa Keys from the Kansas State Historical Society; Rebekah Curry from Emporia State University; Cliff Hight, from Kansas State University; Gary Cox, from the University of Missouri; John Dubuisson of the Combined Arms Research Library; Kevin Drewelow, Director of Combat Air Museum; Megan Sims and Anne A. Tangeman of KU's Biodiversity Institute and Natural History Museum; Bethany Mowry, formerly of the University Press of Kansas, my first editor; Kat Trueman-Gardener, an awesome artist and the best childminder we've ever had; photographer Steve Puppe; Cathy Jarzemkoski, Brian Carpenter, and Missy Minear, for their assistance with mascot information and photos; Amy Hurst, the first Baby Jay, for sharing her story and photographs; Anthony W. Walton, from the Department of Geology; the Standing family, for donating that amazing quilt; Steve Johnson and Shaun Harris, who were kind enough to open up the Jayhawk Tower and Theatre to us; Robert Farha, owner of The Wheel; Summer Foster, KU Marketing; Kim LaFever and Leah Nicholson, from Academic Success; Mike Rounds and Mark Reiske, for information on the Protect KU campaign; Larry Pearson, for allowing me to reproduce the cover of his book; Paul Vander Tuig, for his help with licensing information; and finally Joyce Harrison, Kelly Chrisman Jacques, Karl Janssen, Derek Helms, Alec Loganbill, Penelope Cray, and others at the University Press of Kansas who made this book a reality.

1 Origin of the Jayhawk and the Rock Chalk Yell

The Jayhawk is one of the United States' most historical and identifiable university mascots. It is unique among other mascots—including animals such as tigers, bulldogs, and wildcats; objects such as cyclones and wheat shocks; and people such as the Ichabods and the Demon Deacons—because it has been evolving for more than a hundred years and that evolutionary process has been so well documented. The Jayhawk has its roots in the establishment of the state of Kansas and symbolizes much more than a university mascot. Today, the Jayhawk is deeply associated with the struggles of those who founded the University of Kansas and remains at the heart of the university.

Documented references trace the first use of the term "jayhawker" to the California gold rush of 1848. In *The Jayhawkers' Oath and Other Sketches* (1949), William Lewis Manly locates the term's origin in the group of men he traveled with from Illinois to the California gold fields: "When the party of ambitious young men referred to had crossed the Missouri River, near where Omaha now stands, and were journeying up the Platte Valley, it occurred to them that their caravan should have a name, and then and there they dubbed themselves the 'Jayhawkers.'"[1] John B. Colton, another member of the party, describes the jayhawk as a bird of prey: "Some kind of hawks, as they sail up in the air reconnoitering for mice and other small prey, look and act as though they were the whole thing. Then the audience of jays and other small but jealous and vicious birds sail in and jab him, until he gets tired of show life and slides out of trouble in the lower earth."[2]

Another version of the origin of the term "Jayhawker" relates more closely to early Kansas. In 1856, before the start of the Civil War, several bloody skirmishes along the territorial border broke out between raiders from both the Kansas Territory and Missouri. One of those raiders was Patrick Devlin, an Irish immigrant and arguably the most important person in the history of the term. Separate accounts from three Kansas counties along the Missouri border—Miami, Linn, and Bourbon—each credit Devlin with first using the word, in this case as a verb, "Jayhawking." All three accounts are remarkably alike and describe Pat Devlin returning from raids with plundered household goods slung across his mule. The following version hails from Osawatomie, Miami County: "Before the sun was up, one morning in the fall of 1856, a free-stater, named Pat Devlin, was seen riding into town on a well-loaded mule. A neighbor remarked, 'Pat, you look like you had been on an excursion.' Pat answered that he had been 'Jayhawking.' Asked for an explanation, Pat said he had been foraging off the enemy; that in Ireland, a bird called the jayhawk worried its prey before devouring it. From this incident, we have the now familiar name of Jayhawker."[3]

One of the well-known military figures to carry the moniker of Jayhawker is Dr. Charles R. Jennison. As A. T. Andreas relates in *History of the State of Kansas* (1883), "the word [Jayhawk] became generally known during the War of the Rebellion from the application of it to himself and his soldiers by Col. Jennison of the Seventh Kansas. From his regiment it passed to all Kansas soldiers, and finally was applied to the inhabitants of Kansas themselves."[4]

Poster calling volunteers to join Colonel Jennison's "Independent Kansas Jay-Hawkers."

A carte de visite of Colonel Charles R. Jennison (probably 1861).

For many years after the Civil War, "Jayhawker" was used to generally refer to people living in Kansas. Indeed, as late as 1935, people across the state considered themselves to be Jayhawkers. *The Jayhawker Book: A Book of Kansas for Little Kansans*, by Emma Humble, an associate professor of education at Kansas State Teachers College, Emporia, was so popular that it was reprinted seven times between 1935 and 1998. Laura M. French, in an article published in the *Emporia Gazette* on January 29, 1935—Kansas Day, no less—described the book as an "enchanting foundation for later study of Kansas history" and its cover as "bound in sunflower yellow and green, with the cut of the Jolly Jayhawk . . . bringing in red and blue tones." The article continues, "Nothing like this book has ever been written for kindergarten and primary instruction, and as a textbook it would be invaluable."[5] The popular book served to teach children across the state that they were Jayhawkers into the 1990s.

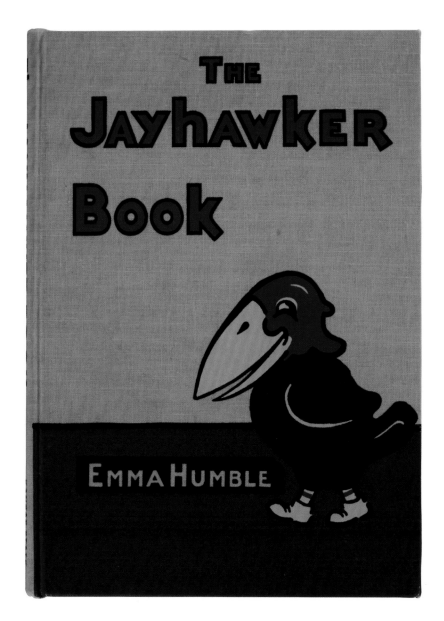

The cover and pages from Emma Humble's *The Jayhawker Book,* seventh reprint, 1998. The book was originally published in 1935.

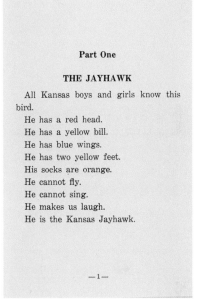

Part One

THE JAYHAWK

All Kansas boys and girls know this bird.

He has a red head.

He has a yellow bill.

He has blue wings.

He has two yellow feet.

His socks are orange.

He cannot fly.

He cannot sing.

He makes us laugh.

He is the Kansas Jayhawk.

—1—

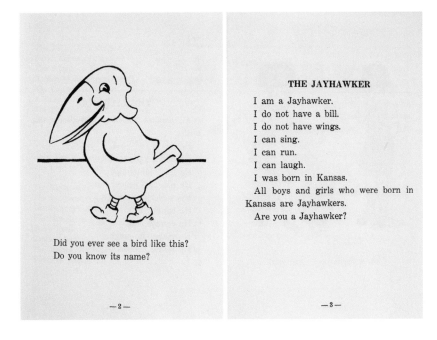

Did you ever see a bird like this?
Do you know its name?

—2—

THE JAYHAWKER

I am a Jayhawker.

I do not have a bill.

I do not have wings.

I can sing.

I can run.

I can laugh.

I was born in Kansas.

All boys and girls who were born in Kansas are Jayhawkers.

Are you a Jayhawker?

—3—

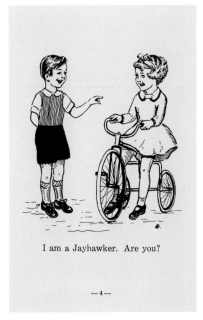

I am a Jayhawker. Are you?

—4—

The earliest association of the term "Jayhawk" with the University of Kansas appears in the "Rock Chalk, Jay Hawk" college yell. During the mid-nineteenth century, college yells were an integral part of the student experience around the country. Most colleges had an institution-wide yell or chant, and classes and clubs often had yells as well. In 1886, when the Rock Chalk yell was created, the university had been in operation for only twenty years, and KU students had yet to develop the sense of community identity that students in older colleges and universities enjoyed. The student body's adoption of the yell was among the first signs of the burgeoning student unity that would become an enduring university tradition.

In 1891, the university celebrated its twenty-fifth anniversary with the publication of a quarter-centennial history. Included were chapters on the history of KU and its most illustrious faculty. Professor of French Arthur G. Canfield wrote the chapter on KU student life and concluded with enthusiastic recognition of the importance of the Rock Chalk yell:

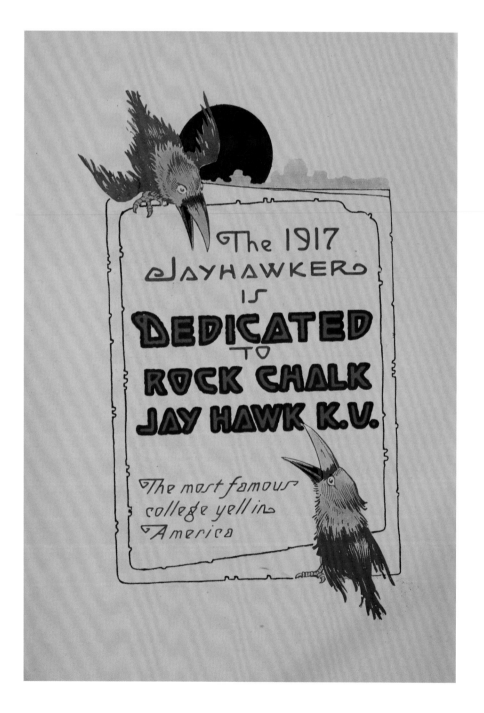

Dedication page of the 1917 *Jayhawker*.

"No one can well doubt the vigorous loyalty of the student body to the University when he hears the thunder of the college yell sent up from the foot-ball or base-ball field. The existence of the yell itself is a proof of that spirit; one common sentiment of love and pride and exultation seeks expression in one common form of words—'Rock Chalk, Jay Hawk, K.U.'"[6]

Professor E. H. S. Bailey of the Department of Chemistry, the self-proclaimed creator of the Rock Chalk yell, describes the yell as originating with a university science club in 1886. In "How and When 'Rock Chalk' Came into Being," published in the 1917 *Jayhawker* yearbook, which was dedicated to "Rock Chalk Jay Hawk K.U. The most famous college yell in America," Professor Bailey describes how it was at one of the science club meetings that the idea to adopt a yell began:

> Shortly after this meeting, early one morning, I was thinking of the matter of these words [and it] occurred to me; "Rah, Rah, Jay Hawk, K.U." three times repeated, with staccato emphasis. . . . By some process of evolution, and I think at the suggestion of some of the Snow Hall men, the "Rah, Rah" was changed to "Rock Chalk," and finally in the enthusiasm of the early football days, the long roll twice repeated was substituted for the first part of the slogan. And so the yell "that sounds o'er land and sea" was introduced into K.U.[7]

The new science club yell became so popular that it was used just one year later, in 1887, at the state oratorical contest in Topeka. During the late nineteenth and early twentieth centuries, oratorical contests between local colleges were almost as popular as sporting events. In his wonderful history of KU, *The Years on Mount Oread*, Robert Taft recounts finding the earliest printed version of the famous yell in the *University Courier*, a student newspaper:

> At the end of a paragraph (February 4, 1887) which attempted to work up enthusiasm for the [oratorical] contest, appeared the words "Rock-Chock-Jay Hawk-K.U." The yell was still so new to the reporter that the significance of the second word was not realized! By the next fall however, it was known to all as the property of the whole University, for the *Courier* on November 4, 1887 reads: "Every college of importance in this country has a college cry. In every town in which a college is situated, the midnight air resounds with the hideous yells of the student, symbolic of victory, defeat, or devilment."[8]

In the December 1890 issue of another student periodical, the *University Review*, students were urged to support the contestants by sending a big delegation to the oratorical contest in Emporia and to "let those omnipotent, irrepressible *Rock-chalks* cleave a victorious welkin." In the same issue of the *University Review*, the editor eloquently pokes fun at the University of Missouri for not having a yell:

> We feel rather sorry for Missouri State University—she has no college yell. It would be pretty hard for the average K. S. U. student to conceive of a college without this necessary requisite. What becomes of all that pent up enthusiasm of students on great occasions? A great part of it is certainly lost, and it must inevitably fade away before that unified and forcible effort which is "breathed" out in a well concerted "yell." When *Rock-chalk Jay-hawk K. U!!* leaps forth and bumps against the blue sky, and crawls along the ground, and sets the atmosphere in rapid vibration—there is an inexpressible thrill seizes the breast of the hearer;

Rock Chalk, Jay Hawk, K. U.

How and When "Rock Chalk" Came into Being

WE must go back more than thirty years to learn about the beginnings of our famous yell, the "Rock Chalk" of which we are so proud. In the year 1883-'4 a Science club was started by some of the older men of the University, including Dr. E. L. Nichols, now head of the Physics department of Cornell University; Doctor Snow, the late chancellor; Professor Marvin, the late dean of the School of Engineering; E. Miller, of California, emeritus professor of Mathematics and Astronomy; and the writer, who was professor of Chemistry.

None of the above departments were at that time strong enough to support a seminar or department club, as there were only three hundred students in the University proper. Consequently the Science Club was started as a clearing house for scientific information, and also to keep the students of the sciences together. At its weekly meetings papers were read and the social side of the club was not neglected. There was an annual Science Club day, with a social gathering in the evening, and the scientific work of the year was reviewed by professors and advanced students; there were excursions to Blue Mound, Leavenworth or Kansas City. As the ladies were always in the company, these trips were very popular.

Perhaps the most famous of the "doings" of the Science Club was the unique annual banquet, known as the "It," a name proposed by Professor Martin, after we had sought in vain for an appropriate name for such a feast of jollity and wit. This was attended by members only and held in the basement of the Chemistry building, now Medical Hall. The "It" recalls many pleasant memories to the students of the Nineties. Usually after an oyster supper prepared by the expert cooks of the club, a program was "put on." The speakers told of their own discoveries (?) and burlesqued those of their colleagues.

This may seem a long introduction to the history of "Rock Chalk" but as it was originally designed for the sole use and profit of the Science Club, this seems proper. It was at one of our meetings in 1887 or '88, over our doughnuts and cider, that someone suggested that we adopt a yell. Several were presented to the club, tried and found unsatisfactory. Shortly after this meeting, early one morning, I was thinking of the matter of these words occurred to me: "Rah, Rah, Jay Hawk, K. U." three times repeated, with staccato emphasis. I proposed this yell at the next meeting of the club and it was adopted. We used it with such success on our picnics and excursions that it was soon taken up by the student body at large and made the regular yell of the University. Shortly after this, by some process of evolution, and I think at the suggestion of some of the Snow Hall men, the "Rah, Rah" was changed to "Rock Chalk," and finally in the enthusiasm of the early football days, the long roll twice repeated was substituted for the first part of the slogan. And so the yell "that sounds o'er land and sea" was introduced into K. U.—*Prof. E. H. S. Bailey.*

6

and immediately another *Rock-chalk* springs into existence and—dear M. U. we would advise you to get a yell.[9]

Just as important as the words of the yell are its rhythm and cadence. In recent years, students have attempted to change the cadence of the chant, but these on-the-fly alterations have been resisted. An early history of the yell's cadence is found in a small booklet, titled "Basketball at the. . . . University of Kansas," published in 1936:

> As yelled by the Science Club, before being taken over for general university use in 1887, the "Rock Chalk," was "Rah, Rah! Jayhawk KU!" given three times with a quick staccato accent.

The account continues:

> By 1899 constant usage of the yell had developed a new technique. In lieu of the staccato accent, the first three lines (which then had been changed to two) were given more slowly and drawn out into the present day "Rock-Chalk-Jayhawk-K.U." But even then the "K.U." at the end was given quickly. It was not until about 1905 that the students and fans began elongating the "K" and the "U," adding the intonation of three steps down the scale on the "U." To the two elongated lines were added three short staccato lines, thus putting the final touches to what today is the most famous yell in America.

Thus we have:

ROCK CHALK, JAYHAWK, K.U.
ROCK CHALK, JAYHAWK, K.U.
       ROCK CHALK! JAYHAWK! K.U.!
       ROCK CHALK! JAYHAWK! K.U.!
       ROCK CHALK! JAYHAWK! K.U.![10]

Much debated over the years are the origin and meaning of the term "Rock Chalk." One often-repeated theory is that the term originated in the belief that the university is physically built on chalk. The debate has been going on for so long that associate professor of geology Anthony Walton, who taught an introductory geology field course from 1998 to 2019, incorporated the discussion into his teaching. In his guidebook for the class, he points out that the KU campus is actually built on limestone, not chalk, and he incorporates another story of the chant: "A geology field trip to central or western Kansas, where chalk—Rock Chalk—is so common, was a key stage in development of the chant and that geologists played a part in its development. Any long field trip in the late nineteenth century depended on rail transportation to cover ground quickly. Perhaps the story about Dr. Bailey and the chant in 1886 is true, but *rock chalk* replaced *rah rah* on a Geology field trip as the locomotive pulled out of the station."[11] Certainly, geology professor Francis Snow, a founding member of the science club, would have been well aware of the geology of western Kansas. It is quite possible that Professor Snow is the source of the strange words.

The yell made its first appearance in the university annuals in the *Helianthus* of 1889. In a small essay titled "Science, Psychology & Rock Chalk," drawings of an "old professor" giving the yell with student-like fervor cut two diagonal lines through the text.

Facing page: The "How and When 'Rock Chalk' Came into Being" page of the 1917 *Jayhawker*.

Examples of yells from the classes of 1899 through 1902 are printed in the 1899 *Oread*, another predecessor to the *Jayhawker*. The yell for the class of 1900 was "We know it all, We can't be taught, Rock Chalk, Jayhawk, Class of Naughty Naught!" Many of the yells incorporated the words "Rock Chalk," "Jayhawk," and "KU" in some fashion.

The old professor
chants, 1889
Helianthus, 81.

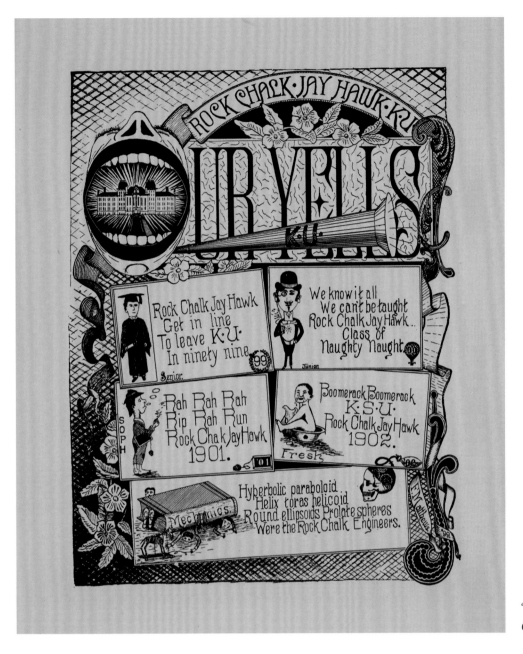

The "Rock Chalk" yell was often touted as being world-famous. There are multiple examples of the yell being given in different parts of the world, but the earliest may belong to the Twentieth Kansas soldiers who, under KU graduate General Frederick Funston's command, used the chant while fighting on battlefronts in the Philippine Islands in 1899. Their war cry was slightly different, as they used "Rock Chalk Jayhawk K V," for the Kansas Volunteers.

Kansas soldiers carried the yell as they fought in wars throughout the twentieth century. It was heard in trenches during World War I and repeated during World War II. It was reportedly chanted at the 1920 Summer Olympics in Antwerp when the nobility wanted to hear a typical American college yell. The assembled athletes agreed that "Rock Chalk, Jayhawk" from the University of Kansas should receive that honor. KU student Everett L. Bradley won a silver medal in the pentathlon in the Antwerp Olympics, so we know there was a KU presence at those Olympic Games. Theodore Roosevelt visited Lawrence several times, in 1903 and twice in 1910, and is said to have called the Rock Chalk yell the greatest college cheer in America.

Right: Drawing from *Leslie's Weekly*. Caption reads "Colonel Funston leading his dashing Kansans, with their thrilling war-cry, "Rock Chalk, Jay-Hawk! K.V.! Kansas Volunteers."

Below: Yell leaders in 1923 very cleverly had the yell printed on the back of their sweaters. From the 1924 *Jayhawker*, 138.

COLONEL FUNSTON LEADING HIS DASHING KANSANS, WITH THEIR THRILLING WAR-CRY, "ROCK, CHALK, JAY-HAWK! K.V.! KANSAS VOLUNTEERS!"—*Drawn for "Leslie's Weekly."*
by *Howard Chandler Christy.*

The words to the yell were literally written in stone in 1901 as the Dyche Hall of Natural History was being constructed. Sculptor Joseph Robaldo Frazee carved twelve grotesques from Cottonwood limestone for the outside of the building. Leonard Krishtalka, director emeritus of the KU Biodiversity Institute & Natural History Museum, believes that the sculptures were meant to be guardians of the natural world, as represented by the museum. On three of the imposing animal figures are chiseled the words "Rock Chalk" (elephant), "J Hawk ?" (rhinoceros), and "KU" (bat/winged dragon). The reason for the question mark on the "J Hawk" shield remains a mystery. No extant records provide an explanation, but one suggestion is that what appears to be a question mark may in fact be merely a decorative design.

The grotesques being chiseled during the building of Dyche Hall, 1901–1902.

Concern about the stability of the more-than-a-century-old stone grotesques prompted an effort in 2019 to save the original statues. They were removed from the outside of the building and placed inside the museum for protection. Sculptors have since completed new grotesques, which were placed in the original positions in 2022. The original grotesques are now part of a display on the sixth floor of the KU Natural History Museum.

Perhaps the most credit for extending the Jayhawk myth should be granted to Frank Wilson Blackmar, a former KU professor and dean of the Graduate School. In "What the Jayhawk Stands For," a six-minute radio talk that also appeared as an essay in December 1926, Blackmar reminds listeners of the origin of the Jayhawk, a creature he describes as a myth that "has no historical use." That myth, Blackmar explains, "had its rise in the characters of two birds that frequent the Missouri Valley, namely the blue jay, a noisy, quarrelsome, robber [of other birds' nests] . . . and the sparrow hawk, a genteel killer of birds, rats, mice and rabbits, and when necessary a courageous and cautious fighter." He shares that originally "jayhawking" was a "general term to express marauding or plundering" before it eventually came to represent Kansans and the University of Kansas. Artists' attempts to express the

mythical bird ranged "all the way from a 'dicky-bird' with a huge bill, wearing boots, to a disconsolate crow, and to a fierce looking fighting bird." This last reference may be to the "fierce looking" Jayhawks drawn on multiple athletic programs of the time, since the first official fierce Jayhawk didn't appear on the KU stage until 1929.

Blackmar ends with a flourish, declaring: "But no matter about the origin of this mythical creature, about its uncertain history, about its early use by people whose actions were sometimes questionable; today 'Jayhawk' embodies the Kansas spirit, the University spirit of unity, loyalty, honesty and right living."[12]

In 1936, the Kansas Alumni Association republished Blackmar's speech in the February issue of the *Graduate Magazine*, refocusing public attention on the mythic bird. In August 1942, the speech was published once more, in the *Kansas Business Magazine*.

Today, Allen Fieldhouse, one of the greatest venues for college basketball, features the Rock Chalk chant as one of the signature elements of its reputation. Joining the masses of KU fans in the rolling cadence of the chant as it echoes through the huge building is a truly special experience. The Fieldhouse even holds the Guinness World Record for loudest crowd roar. As Lauren Hawkins wrote in a special insert to the *Daily Kansan* on March 4, 2019, "The chant is what ties fans together, intentionally connecting the crowd before games. Joining the tradition and KU community is enough to remind anyone, there is truly no place like home."

Facing page: The "Rock Chalk" elephant grotesque on the south side of Dyche Hall.

Above: The three original grotesques on display in the KU Natural History Museum.

Notes

1. William Lewis Manly, *The Jayhawkers' Oath and Other Sketches* (Los Angeles, CA: Warren F. Lewis, Publisher, 1949), 21.

2. Simeon M. Fox, "The Story of the Seventh Kansas," *Transactions of the Kansas State Historical Society*, vol. 8 (Topeka: Kansas State Historical Society, 1904), 13–49, quote from footnote 17.

3. "Osawatomie History," Family Histories and Stories of Miami County, Kansas (Paola, KS: Miami County Historical Society, 1987), 30.

4. "Jayhawkers, the Origin of the Name," *History of the State of Kansas* (Chicago: A. T. Andreas, 1883), II, 878. I used the 1976 reprint.

5. Laura M. French, "The Jayhawker Book," *Emporia Gazette*, January 29, 1935.

6. Arthur G. Canfield, "Student Life in K.S.U.," in *Quarter-Centennial History of the University of Kansas, 1866–1891*, ed. Wilson Sterling (Topeka, KS: Geo. W. Crane & Co., 1891), 157.

7. E. H. S. Bailey, "How and When 'Rock Chalk' Came into Being," *Jayhawker* (Lawrence: University of Kansas, 1917), 10.

8. Robert Taft, "Rock Chalk, Jay Hawk!," *The Years on Mount Oread* (Lawrence: University of Kansas Press, 1955), 29.

9. "Editorial," *University Review* 12, no. 4 (December 1890): 121–122.

10. "The Greatest College Yell in America," K.U. News Bureau, *Basketball at the . . . University of Kansas* (Lawrence, KS: KU Physical Education Corporation, 1936), 11.

11. Anthony W. Walton, "Rock Chalk: Chalk, Marl, the Cretaceous, and Jayhawks," classroom lecture.

12. F. W. Blackmar, "Origin of the Jayhawk: Six Minute Radio Talk" (Lawrence, KS: University of Kansas, 1926).

2 THE EVOLUTION OF THE JAYHAWK

From the 1890s to the start of the twentieth century, football was king at the University of Kansas, as it was at many other colleges and universities across the country. The university also fielded a baseball team, but the sport did not receive nearly as much attention as football; basketball had just been invented by Dr. James Naismith in 1891 and would not be played at KU until Naismith arrived on campus in 1898.

Less than five years after the Rock Chalk yell connected the word "Jayhawk" to the University of Kansas, KU's athletic teams had become known as Jayhawkers. Yet it would be almost two more decades before personifications of the Jayhawk as an actual bird materialized.

During the first decade of the 1900s, drawings of Jayhawks began to appear in publications about KU football. In a cartoon from the 1908 *Jayhawker* yearbook, a pterodactyl-like Jayhawk, drawn by C. W. Lusk, sits on a goalpost cackling at a very woebegone Missouri Tiger on the ground below. The Tiger's tail is in knots, with the dates of KU football victories against Missouri displayed on tags for all to see.

One of the more unusual early Jayhawks appeared in the college scrapbook of KU student Pauline Madden, who attended KU from 1901 to 1909. Taped to a page is a triangle of red paper with a string (perhaps it was intended to hang from a button?). On the tag, a Jayhawk seems to fly through the air with a pig in his talons. Also on the page is a photograph of the 1909 football team with a pig sprawled on the ground in front of the lined-up men. The pig, named Don Carlos, was owned by one of the team's coaches, and each member of the team contributed to the upkeep of this particular team mascot.

Image of the Jayhawk and the Missouri Tiger from the 1908 *Jayhawker*, 159.

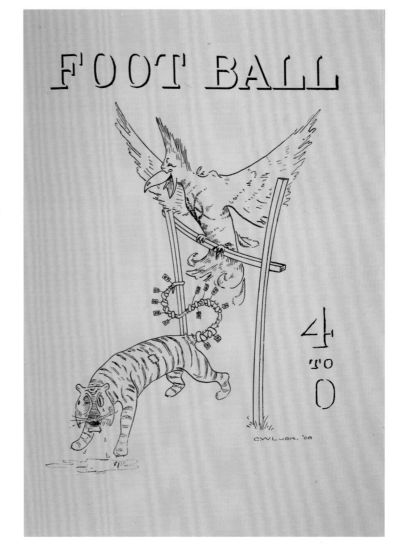

15

Pauline Madden's
student scrapbook,
1909, 35.

On November 24, 1910, KU and Missouri met on the football field for their annual Thanksgiving Day contest. A Jayhawk appeared on the football game program for that game and in the November 25, 1910, issue of the *Kansas City Journal*. This Jayhawk had a substantial beak and feet that look somewhat like the feet of a turkey. In the imaginative cartoon that accompanied the newspaper story about the game, a turkey is shown perched on top of a post to which both the Missouri Tiger and the KU Jayhawk are tied. The game ended in a 5–5 tie that year.

Left: Cartoon from
the November 25,
1910, *Kansas City
Journal*, 9, and found
in the scrapbook of
KU student Streeter
Blair, 10.

Right: Program for
the Thanksgiving Day
football game, 1910.

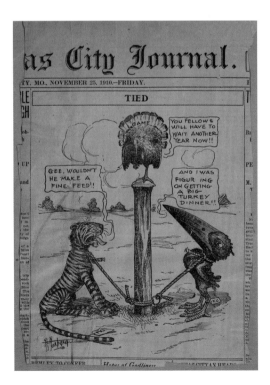

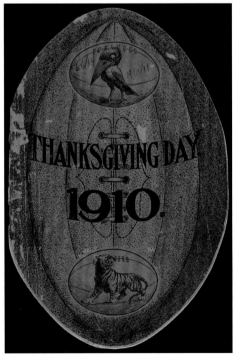

THE 1912 JAYHAWK

The first Jayhawk to become serialized was created by KU undergraduate Daniel Henry "Hank" Maloy in 1912. This Jayhawk is acknowledged as the true first Jayhawk, because Maloy continued to draw it over and over again, and it appeared in print many times. In 2012, the university celebrated the centennial of this version of the Jayhawk.

DANIEL HENRY MALOY,   .   .   .   A. B.
Eureka.

Skull and K, Daily Kansan Board (3-4),
Art Editor 1912 and 1913 Jayhawkers,
Secy.-Treas. Men's Student Council (4),
Treas. Junior Class (3), Treas. Senior
Class (4).

Senior picture of
Daniel Henry Maloy,
1914 *Jayhawker*, 72.

The story of how Maloy conceived of his Jayhawk appeared in an article in the November 21, 1944, *Kansas City Times*. As a freshman in 1910, Maloy was a frustrated artist who continually tried to get his drawings into the *University Daily Kansan*, the student newspaper. In 1911, Merle Thorpe in the School of Journalism saw Maloy's drawings and recognized his talent. He called Maloy into his office and suggested that he continue to work out a cartoon strip each week, promising that he would use his influence to see that they were printed in the *Kansan*. Maloy finished his sophomore year with renewed hope for his cartoonist ambitions. As to the origin of Maloy's Jayhawk, the 1944 *Times* article stated that the next year, when Maloy was a junior and out walking down Massachusetts Street, he, "quite by accident, spotted a stuffed chicken hawk in the window of Con Squire's photographic studio. Now Maloy all the time had been thinking that the word 'jayhawk' in the yell 'rock chalk, jayhawk' was a verb. When jayhawkers go jayhawking they jayhawk, he deduced. He began to meditate on the word 'jayhawk' for a minute or two as he stared into the window." He then went to his home at 930 Illinois Street and started to draw. Maloy said that he erased the drawing so many times the paper started to get thin.

The result of his work was the iconic cartoon of a bird with long, human-like legs and big boots. The 1944 article continued, "He came to an impasse when he found that a bird's knees bent the wrong way for his purpose—it could only kick backwards like a mule. Laboring on into the night he finally solved the problem by simply putting a man's legs and shoes on the jayhawk. And so there it was, the first lusty artistic infant that was to grow up to make history at K.U."

The first Jayhawk Maloy drew was published in the October 28, 1912, *University Daily Kansan*. Years later, Maloy explained that even though this Jayhawk was the second Jayhawk cartoon to appear in print, he actually drew it first. The Jayhawk is wearing big boots and demonstrating its kicking ability against the Kansas State Agricultural College (now Kansas

State University) Aggies. There was a popular song at the time, "They Gotta Quit Kickin' My Dawg Aroun'," and Maloy drew this cartoon to reflect that sentiment. The notes written on these cartoons are in Maloy's hand. (The song was written by Byron G. Harlan in 1912 and can be found on YouTube.)

Even though it was drawn first, this Maloy Jayhawk was not the first one to appear in print. That honor belongs to the cartoon that appeared three days earlier, in the October 25, 1912, issue of the *University Daily Kansan*. That Jayhawk is shown shooing away Jinx, a small catlike creature, also drawn by Maloy, that was blamed for football losses and other calamities.

The first Jayhawk cartoon drawn by Hank Maloy, *University Daily Kansan*, October 28, 1912.

The first Jayhawk to appear in print, *University Daily Kansan*, October 25, 1912.

During his sophomore year in 1911, Maloy drew illustrations for the *Jayhawker* yearbook, and during his junior and senior years he served as a staff member on both the *Jayhawker* and the *University Daily Kansan*. Besides the Jayhawk and Jinx, he drew other characters, including Faculty Man, a short, portly gentleman with whiskers, and Mother KU, who wore an apron and spectacles. The 1913 *Jayhawker* featured a plethora of Maloy cartoons. Nine pages of drawings, titled "Milestones We Passed This Year," included Jinx oiling his steamroller, Faculty Man carrying off a turkey for Thanksgiving, a student battling the "EXAM" dragon, and other characters concerned about the KU budget.

In a comic strip published in the *UDK* on September 30, 1913, Maloy introduced his cast of cartoon characters, as well as drawings of himself as a *Kansan* cartoonist, to the new class of freshmen. In this drawing the Jayhawk is shown with its legs crossed. Years later, in a story in the November 1971 *Kansas Alumni* magazine, Maloy explains that he drew the Jayhawk that way because "Mutt and Jeff," characters in a popular comic strip of the time, stood with their legs crossed.

Facing page: Cartoon page drawn by Hank Maloy from the 1913 *Jayhawker*, 398.

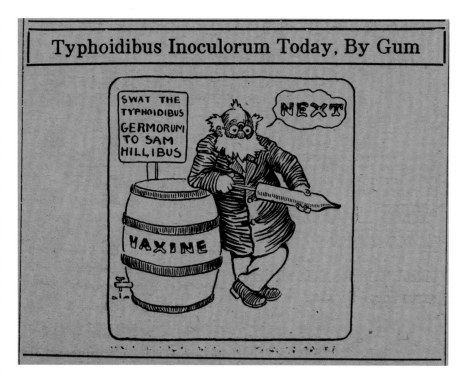

Typhoidibus Inoculorum Today, By Gum

Left: Maloy drew himself in the September 30, 1913, issue of the *University Daily Kansan*.

Above: Cartoon that appeared in the *University Daily Kansan* on November 3, 1914.

Right: William Jennings Bryan caricature that appeared in the January 5, 1914, *University Daily Kansan*.

Mother KU did not survive long, but Faculty Man, as well as Jinx, appeared regularly in Maloy's cartoons for the next few years. In November 1914, Maloy enlisted Faculty Man's assistance in a campaign encouraging students to receive the typhoid vaccine KU was offering at the time.

During Maloy's career as cartoonist for the *Daily Kansan*, his work caught the eye of US Secretary of State William Jennings Bryan. Bryan visited KU on January 5, 1914, and in honor of the visit Maloy drew him into a cartoon that appeared in that day's issue of the *UDK*. When Bryan saw it, he asked to meet the artist. He praised Maloy's work, tore out the picture, and said he would send it to his wife to show her how he looked out in Kansas. In the lower right side of the drawing, a small figure with a megaphone shouts, "All right now everybody in on 'What's the matter with William.'" Maloy is referring to the 1896 newspaper editorial "What's the Matter with Kansas?" written by well-known newspaper publisher, William Allen White from Emporia, Kansas. The editorial criticized presidential candidate William Jennings Bryan, whose populist platform advocated for the free silver standard.

After he graduated, Maloy worked as a front man for the Radcliffe Chautauqua Company. He made bookings and hotel reservations and helped with setup, even doing drawings for the shows. During the latter part of the nineteenth and the early part of the twentieth centuries, the Chautauqua movement flourished in the United States and Canada. The Radcliffe Chautauqua Company, which toured the country, advertised a "Big Community Festival . . . Three Afternoons and Evenings of Novelty Entertainments, Eloquent Addresses, Good Music, Clean, Wholesome and Inspirational, with Special Features for Children."

Maloy served in the army during World War I, and after his release, he returned to his hometown of Eureka, where he joined the *Eureka Democratic Messenger* as editor, cartoonist, and printer. Maloy remained in Eureka for eighteen years before returning to Lawrence in 1952 to work on the *Lawrence Outlook* newspaper. Throughout his life, he continued to draw

CHAUTAUQUA

Hank Maloy can be seen on the right drawing a cartoon character on the side of a tent, 1915. From the Henry Maloy scrapbook.

the Jayhawk and had an ongoing relationship with the Alumni Association. For instance, from 1965 until 1971, the year of his death, he drew Jayhawk Christmas cartoons that appeared in the *Alumni Magazine*. Among his papers in the University Archives are sketches, Christmas cards, and invitations. There is even an undated sketch of "hippy" Jayhawks with long hair and headbands marching and carrying peace signs.

A cartoon strip of busy Maloy Jayhawks from the *Lawrence Outlook* (date unknown).

The November 1971 issue of the *Kansas Alumni* magazine was a celebration of Maloy's life. The cover photo showed Maloy riding bikes with Big Jay. Even at the age of seventy-nine, Maloy was known to ride his bike everywhere. He answered the invitation for the photo shoot by saying, "Sounds goofy but I go in for anything goofy like that." Sadly, Hank Maloy died just two weeks after riding with Big Jay.

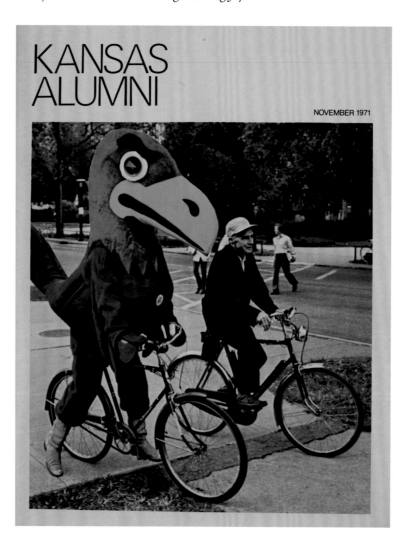

Cover of the November 1971 issue of the *Kansas Alumni*.

The 1920 Jayhawk

The somber bird perched on a KU monogram, known as the 1920 and the second signature Jayhawk, first appeared in the October 1921 issue of the KU Alumni Association's *Graduate Magazine* and may have been designed by a member of the magazine staff. The bird was used to advertise *Life at Laurel Town in Anglo-Saxon Kansas*, a newly published book by Kate Stephens described as "a Book All K. U. Will Enjoy, the Jayhawker Spirit into Print." Stephens graduated from KU in 1876, a member of the university's fourth graduating class.

The November 1921 issue of *Graduate Magazine* has another interesting Jayhawk on its cover, this one depicted within a shield. A short description explains the image: "There is interesting significance in the central figure which is a conventionalized picture of the famed K.U. yell 'Rock Chalk Jayhawk, K.U.'" This image appeared only a few times in the magazine.

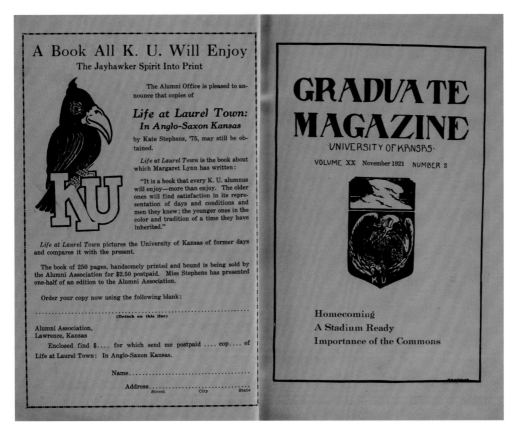

Above: October 1921 *Graduate Magazine* with the 1920 Jayhawk advertising a book by Kate Stephens. The facing page is the cover of the November 1921 issue of the *Graduate Magazine*.

Right: *Graduate Magazine*, November 1921, 17.

— K. U. —

THE new cover for the Graduate Magaine this month has been designed by William M. Hekking, professor in the School of Fine Arts. There is interesting significance in the central figure, which is a conventionalized picture of the famed K. U. yell 'Rock Chalk Jayhawk, K. U." Profesor Hekking's conception of the Jayhawk is a bird in action. By close study of the design one notices that the Jayhawk bill holds the striped tail of a Tiger, symbolizing the ancient rivalry between Missouri and Kansas Universities. It takes slight stretch of the imagination to find the "Rock Chalk" portion of the picture at the top. At the bottom is the concluding "K. U."

— K. U. —

A variation of the 1920 Jayhawk appeared on the cover of the sheet music for "I'm A Jayhawk," a pep song written by George H. "Dumpy" Bowles in 1920. A 1912 graduate, Bowles was president of the KU Club of Kansas City when he wrote the song that is still being sung today.

The Alumni Association was not the only entity to feature the 1920 Jayhawk. The Athletics Department used it several times for their publications. A full color version of this Jayhawk was used in a print advertisement on the back cover of a 1922 football program.

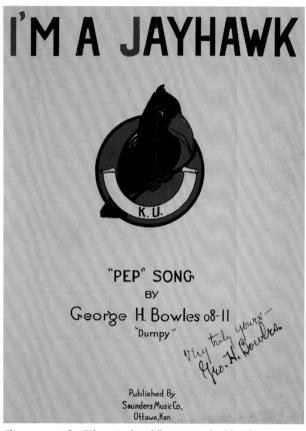

Sheet music for "I'm a Jayhawk" autographed by the song-writer, George H. Bowles.

Back cover of a 1922 football program.

THE 1922 JAYHAWK

The next Jayhawk to step onto the KU stage was the "quaint, duck-like" bird drawn by two sophomores, James "Jimmy" Edward O'Bryon and George Phillips Hollingbery, just before the KU–Nebraska game in 1921. Inspired by KU cheerleaders at a pregame football rally, they immediately returned to O'Bryon's home at 1109 Ohio Street and started work. O'Bryon drew the bird and Hollingbery was the sales manager. Once they had their design, they charged money to paint it on the windows of student jalopies going to the game in Nebraska. This endeavor was so successful that they went on to paint their Jayhawk on store windows in downtown Lawrence in preparation for the upcoming football game against the University of Missouri. In an account written in 1931, "The Birth of a Jayhawk," O'Bryon recalls: "It was evident that this new Jayhawk, though retaining some of the characteristics of its predecessors, should be of virginal mould [sic], embodying characteristics that the other seemed to lack. That it should in every way symbolize the institution for which it was to stand was of paramount importance. Proud, though not arrogant, determined of visage, it should be a colorful token of the spirit of Kansas."[1]

Left: James E. O'Bryon, 1924 *Jayhawker*.

Right: George Hollingbery, 1924 *Jayhawker*.

The Hollingbery and O'Bryon Jayhawk from the *History of the Jayhawk* scrapbook compiled by Watson Library staff in 1931. Note the "Copyright 1922 Jayhawk Posters" mark on the Jayhawk's boots.

Although from years later (ca. 1940), a Hollingbery-O'Bryon car (with the Jayhawk painted on the side) must have looked very similar to this one.

Katharine Tinsdale in an article for the *Kansas Alumni* magazine (no. 6, 2000) wrote that Hollingbery's daughters, Betsy Hollingbery Edwards and Deborah Hollingbery Niethammer, recalled that their father and Jimmy wanted to make money by selling the Jayhawk stickers they had created. They stole into the Alumni Association office and stealthily acquired an alumnus mailing list. Then, they contacted everyone on the list offering the stickers for sale. The daughters reported that Hollingbery and O'Bryon earned about $20,000 from their mailing campaign.

Despite its rather goofy appearance, this Jayhawk enjoyed years of fame and success. O'Bryon and Hollingbery copyrighted their Jayhawk in 1922 under their company name, Jayhawk Posters. Large quantities of stickers were printed and sold, and the Jayhawk was used on advertisements for Jayhawk Cleaners and the Gustafson jewelry store. The Fritz Tire Company, the Carter Tire and Supply Company, and the Hotel Jayhawk in Topeka also used this Jayhawk on their advertisements—apparently without permission, since O'Bryon and Hollingbery won a lawsuit against these three businesses in 1929 for copyright infringement.

Forrest C. "Phog" Allen, KU's athletic director at the time, seemed particularly fond of the 1922 Jayhawk, as it was used on KU basketball gear from 1928 through 1950.

After college, O'Bryon and Hollingbery moved their business to Chicago. Jimmy O'Bryon later worked in public relations in Chicago and New York and drew a syndicated comic strip, "Happily Ever After." The comic was carried by nearly thirty papers including the *Los Angeles Times*, the *Washington Post*, and the *Cleveland Plain Dealer*. George Hollingbery was employed as the head of advertising for Hearst Papers and in 1935 started his own company, the George P. Hollingbery Corporation, selling ads nationally for radio and eventually TV.

In the official group of six historical Jayhawks, the O'Bryon/Hollingbery Jayhawk is dated 1923. I base my date of 1921 on the following facts: the KU–Nebraska game took place in 1921; O'Bryon and Hollingbery were identified as sophomores, which accords with their graduation in 1924; their bird was copyrighted in 1922. All of these facts point to the

The KU men's basketball team of 1935–1936 with the 1922 Jayhawk patch on their uniforms.

This variant of the 1922 Jayhawk was produced as an appliqué, circa 1920s.

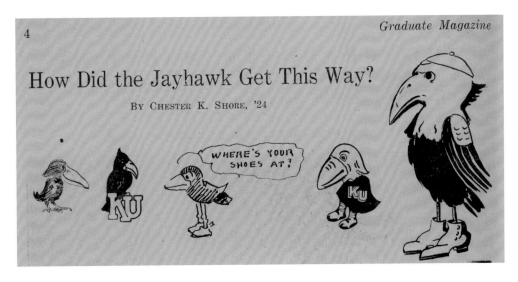

Chester Shore's account of early Jayhawk history from the December 1925 issue of the *Graduate Magazine*. Note the Maloy Jayhawk's question to the 1920 Jayhawk—"Where's your shoes at?"

creation date of 1921 rather than 1923, but in the grand scheme of things, it doesn't really matter, does it? I have split the difference and use the date of copyright, 1922, to date this Jayhawk.

From as early as 1925, KU alumni were interested in how the Jayhawk "evolved." In the December 1925 issue of the Alumni Association *Graduate Magazine*, the article "How Did the Jayhawk Get This Way?," written by Chester K. Shore, appeared with a parade of early Jayhawks at the top of the page. The large Jayhawk at the end wearing a beanie was taken from an advertisement for Ober's Head-to-Foot Out-fitters, a men's clothing store in downtown Lawrence.

This is one of the earliest records of Jayhawk history. Shore recounts stories of the Jayhawk's beginnings, from Pat Devlin's escapades through Maloy's creation to the several different birds used in the early 1920s. He used his article to call for standardization:

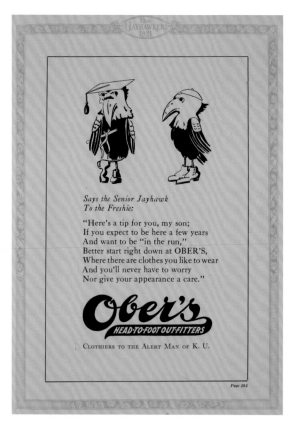

> Get him down so that he will
> have all the good qualities
> of the bird he is. Perhaps a
> composite would do this. Most
> artists picture him as a friendly,
> laughing, awkward bird that
> wears shoes. He should be a
> bird full of fight and serious-
> ness, with claws showing. His
> beak should have the hawk,
> downward curve of a bird of
> prey. He should reflect the ide-
> als of the school and team he
> represents. To do this should
> he look like an overfed duck
> or an alert, fighting bird that
> swoops out upon the world
> with the nerve and power to
> bring home the goods?[2]

The tall Jayhawk portrayed as a "freshie" wearing a beanie from the Shore essay "How Did the Jayhawk Get This Way?" is from an advertisement for Ober's Head-to-Foot Out-fitters in the 1921 *Jayhawker*, 395.

THE 1929 JAYHAWK

Perhaps Shore's call was answered in 1929 by the Jayhawk Club of Kansas City. Their version—drawn by Maclay Lyon Jr., the son of the secretary of the club, Dr. Maclay Lyon, a KU graduate—appeared in print for the first time in an October 11, 1929, *Kansas City Times* article. Lyon Jr. was actually a graduate of the University of Missouri, and his father asked him to "repress his Missouri spirit long enough to create" a Jayhawk who is "militant, rampant, rambunctious and aggressive."

This Jayhawk was in open rebellion against the Jayhawks that came before. The *Times* article described the new mascot as a "tough guy," after its pugilistic stance, with feet planted flat on the floor and spurs like a fighting cock. He was modeled after "Mickey McGuire," a boxer in comedy shorts and a popular cartoon of the time. The club adopted that bird as their official emblem, as Dr. Lyon believed that the "Jayhawk with the smiling countenance and the crossed legs was silly and meaningless." He discussed his opinions with basketball Coach Phog Allen, who told him that he could propose a new design and submit it for approval. Apparently, though, Allen did not like the new Jayhawk. He thought there was too much "swagger and perhaps effrontery about the tough guy."[3]

Although he did not endorse it, Allen also did not discourage Dr. Lyon from submitting his son's Jayhawk for consideration. Not to be deterred, the Jayhawk Club had five thousand stickers of "Mickey Jayhawk" made for distribution at the next football game in Lawrence. Apparently, the Alumni Association and the student body approved of this Jayhawk, because it was used on cheerleader uniforms through the 1930s. At times, the 1922 and the 1929 Jayhawks were used simultaneously.

Tomorrow—Hargiss day at the university—when K. U. plays the Kansas State Teachers' college of Emporia, the hard-boiled boid will make its

JAYHAWK CLUB OF K.C.

THE NEW EMBLEM OF THE KANSAS CITY JAYHAWK CLUB.

The 1929 Jayhawk as it appeared in the October 11, 1929, issue of the *Kansas City Times*.

KU cheerleaders in sweaters with the 1929 Jayhawk patch, 1938–1939.

The Fritz Company copyrighted this appliqué, which looks suspiciously like the 1929 Jayhawk, circa 1930s.

10   *Graduate Magazine*

Discovered: Ancestor of Jayhawkornis Kansasensis

By RAYMOND C. MOORE,
Professor of Geology, University of Kansas

Geologists and many others in the Mid-Continent region of the United States are familiar with the representative of the class Aves called *Jayhawkornis kansasensis*. In the common, more unscientific parlance, this species of bird is familiarly known as the Jayhawk. The Jayhawk is a bird of prey (sometimes spelled pray) that for many years has been very busy alternately seeking to repel barbarian invaders from adjacent country inhabited by the Nebraska Cornhuskers, Missouri Tigers, and Oklahoma Sooners, and then making more or less vicious and successful forays of his own into foreign territory. Occasionally he has made ambitious flights that have carried him as far as the eastern and western coasts. It is not the writer's intent, however, to offer a recondite essay on the habits of the Jayhawk or the nature of his ecological or sociological adaptations. It is our purpose, rather, to call attention to results of recent research on the derivation of this Kansas bird and the nature of his most ancient known progenitor. This takes us into the field of paleontology.

At this point in our study we may direct attention to what has been designated as one of the most famous yells in America, "Rock Chalk, Jayhawk, K. U." a rallying call which with appropriate intonation and enthusiastic volume is familiar to all Kansans and many others. The close association of Jayhawk and rock chalk in this yell certainly directs the attention of an investigator to the possibility that the Cretaceous chalk may contain evidence bearing on the Kansas Jayhawk. There is need for scientific caution, however, in expressing opinion as to whether the association of Jayhawk and chalk suggested the yell or the yell suggested the association. At all events, it is proper to inquire whether there may be avian remains in the chalk beds which may throw light on the lineage of the Jayhawk. Surely, it would be too much to hope that we might discover remains of the original Jayhawk himself, yet nothing seems to be too remarkable for modern science.

As a matter of fact, discovery of the Rock Chalk bird is not at all new. Some of these birds were found as long ago as 1870, when a paleontologic field party from Yale University under direction of Professor O. C. Marsh made first discovery of ancestral Jayhawk bones in the Cretaceous rocks of west-

ern Kansas. Marsh gave to this bird the not unfitting name *Hesperornis regalis*, which means the "kingly western bird." Subsequently other fossil remains have been found, and at the present time there are two remarkably fine mounted skeletons of *Hesperornis* in the Peabody Museum at Yale University, one in the American Museum of Natural History in New York City, one in the National

Skeleton of Hesperornis regalis from the Cretaceous Chalk of Western Kansas

Museum at Washington, and a complete specimen in the Museum of the University of Kansas. A unique feature in connection with the specimen in the University of Kansas collection is the preservation of clear imprints of feathers preserved in the chalk. Thus, we know not only the skeletal form but something of the feather covering that clothed his body. Unfortunately, pigment is rarely preserved in fossils, and consequently we have no actual evidence of the coloring of *Hesperornis*. Under the circumstances, however, is

Restoration of the Ancestral Kansas Rock Chalk Bird

it not reasonable to assume that the red and blue of modern *Jayhawkornis* were the selected hues of the ancient Rock Chalk bird?

Old *Hesperornis* was a good sized bird, the skeleton attaining a length of six feet from tip of beak to end of outstretched toes, and judging from mounted skeletons his height in stocking feet was a good four and a half feet. He was a ferocious-looking bird. We see not only the big strong beak, like that of the modern Jayhawk, but we find that the upper and lower jaws were armed with a row of very sharp-pointed teeth. It is perhaps unfortunate that these teeth, inherited from reptilian ancestors, have been lost in later evolution of the Jayhawk. There are many times when these teeth would come in handy.

In conclusion, it is of interest to point out that the regal birds of the Kansas chalk were very thoroughly adapted to an aquatic life. The modern Jayhawk does fairly well in the water at times, but is better at running and jumping, and has performed well on the football field and basketball floor. The perfection of these different lines of adaptation perhaps signify inherent capacities of the species. It is fortunate or unfortunate, according to point of view, that the fossil remains of the Rock Chalk bird do not permit accurate determination of the size of the brain case, and we cannot, therefore, tell definitely whether there has been considerable development or a decline in intelligence during the course of evolution from *Hesperornis* to *Jayhawkornis*.

Another 14th Street Episode

Mist descended, froze and formed ice on famous old Fourteenth (Adams to old timers) St. (other places too, of course) the afternoon of Jan. 14. Students, faculty, office workers driving cars home that evening did not heed the ice until—the brink was passed. Result: procession of skidding, swaying, whirling, automobiles carrying hysteric but helpless occupants swiftly down the incline. Prof. Carroll D. Clark, '22, in Ford sedan, got as far as Ohio St., where he and passenger, a young sociology instructor, crashed into a tree and broke much glass but nothing more. Jerauld Randall, '35, bounced over the curb at Ohio St., in his Model T Ford which turned on its side. Jerauld's head popped up through the open window still puffing a cigaret. Other cars stopped against telephone poles and other impedimenta along the way, blowing out tires as they jolted over the curb. Such funny sights and sounds attracted a crowd which lingered at the foot of the Hill, no one thinking or caring to go to the top to warn approaching motorists of the danger. Finally some University or city official blockaded the street at Oread Ave., and as night fell red lanterns sent out their cheery glow of warning to keep off Fourteenth St.

Raymond Moore's essay from the April 1932 issue of the *Graduate Magazine.*

A slightly different version of the 1929 Jayhawk was copyrighted by the Fritz Tire Company of Lawrence and sold as appliqués for car windows.

In 1932, esteemed geologist Raymond C. Moore published an essay in the *Graduate Magazine*, "Discovered: Ancestor of Jayhawkornis Kansasensis." In this tongue-in-cheek article, Moore writes that the most ancient known progenitor of "Jayhawkornis Kansasensis" (scientific name for the Jayhawk) is the "Hesperornis regalis," which means the "kingly western bird."

In the essay, he claims that an almost complete skeleton of this Jayhawk ancestor was in the collection of KU's Natural History Museum. The museum does indeed have one of the most complete skeletons of the "Hesperornis regalis," although it is in small pieces and is not a full skeleton resembling the bird in Moore's drawing.

THE 1941 JAYHAWK

The next bird to join the ranks of the six "signature" Jayhawks also displayed a fighting spirit. Drawn by Gene Varner "Yogi" Williams during the summer of 1941, before he had even arrived at KU, this Jayhawk was as militant as the 1929 bird but a bit more refined, with his broader beak, puffed-out chest, and aggressive stance balanced out with a feathered tail and buckles on his shoes. Williams enrolled as a premed student that year but still found time to draw for the *University Daily Kansan*, the *Sour Owl*, a campus humor magazine, and the *Jayhawker*. His "Jayhawk Warrior," as he was sometimes called, was also featured on the 1943 University Calendar along with drawings of his less militant Jayhawks inside. Williams's time at KU was cut short when he entered the military to serve overseas in Europe during World War II as a company aid in the Seventy-First Infantry Division of the Third US Army, although he continued to send drawings to the *Sour Owl*. He returned to KU to study fine arts in 1946 and was welcomed back to the *Jayhawker* as the art editor for the 1947 volume, where he changed the demeanor of his Jayhawk, no longer a warrior but now a happy KU student. In fact, he introduced two new Jayhawks, "Heoweez" and "Heathcliff," to KU students in the fall 1947 issue of the *Jayhawker*. These characters appeared regularly for the next two years in a variety of vignettes.

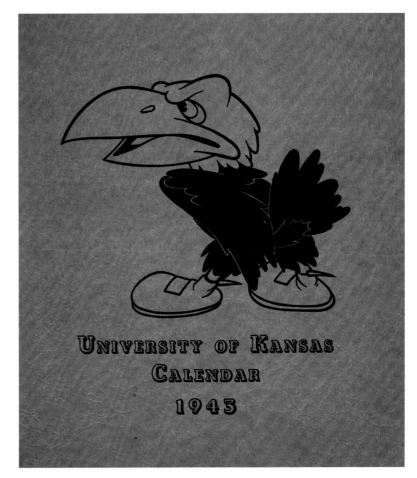

The militant Jayhawk of 1941 drawn by "Yogi" Williams on the cover of the 1943 university calendar.

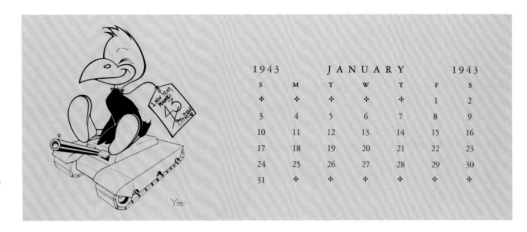

S	M	T	W	T	F	S
✢	✢	✢	✢	✢	1	2
3	4	5	6	7	8	9
10	11	12	13	14	15	16
17	18	19	20	21	22	23
24	25	26	27	28	29	30
31	✢	✢	✢	✢	✢	✢

The January page from the 1943 university calendar with a "Yogi" Williams drawing.

Williams left KU in 1947 and briefly worked in New York City as a commercial artist. He left New York and moved to Taos, New Mexico, where he opened an art studio. He lived with his brother while completing a fine arts degree at the University of New Mexico in 1950. After his brother's death from Hodgkin's disease, he was inspired to study medicine once again. He returned to Kansas in 1950 and acquired his medical degree in 1954. His Dr. and Nurse Jayhawks, drawn for the KU Medical Alumni Association while he was in school and after he graduated, were very popular. They were often produced as stickers and appeared in the Medical School yearbook, the *Jayhawker M.D.*, as well as other publications. Yogi continued to draw while in medical practice in Phoenix and produced yearly Christmas cards with Santa Jayhawks and Jayhawks as cowboys, witches, and grim reapers. He continued to draw for the *Jayhawker M.D.* into the 1960s and produced very striking yearbook covers. He is known for his bronze Jayhawk sculptures as well. In 1979, the KU Alumni Association contracted with Yogi to produce a limited edition of his Jayhawk in bronze. The bronze Jayhawk was nine inches tall and weighed fifteen pounds.

Dr. Williams and his family returned to Kansas in 1970. He died tragically in a hot air balloon accident near his home in El Dorado on July 4, 1979.

As reported in the October 16, 2001, online issue of the *El Dorado Times*, Yogi's Fighting Jayhawk was called once more into service in support of the Families of Freedom Scholarship Fund, a national program that provided scholarships for children and spouses of firefighters and police officers, flight crews and passengers, and World Trade Center and Pentagon workers who were victims of the September 11, 2001, terrorist attacks. An image of Yogi's Jayhawk was printed on T-shirts and sold to support the fund.

Yogi's son, Wade L. Williams, personally donated his father's papers to the University of Kansas Archives in 2013.

"Yogi" Williams's page from the fall 1946 *Jayhawker*, 13.

FALL NUMBER, 1946   13

By Way of Introduction---

The Jayhawker Presents

"*Yogi*" Williams

"Heoweez" and "Heathcliffe"

The Editor had a brainstorm; Yogi Williams had an inspiration; and the 1947 JAYHAWKER has "Heathcliffe and Heoweez."

In the creation of these two new characters, the sky was the limit for no one has ever seen a real Jayhawk. Personifying a bird presents other natural problems and, obviously, no bird, with the one exception of a "chick," ever had a figure anything like Heoweez! As for the exaggeration of the bills, Yogi's only explanation was that he just "likes them that way."

Starting work for the JAYHAWKER back in the fall of 1941, Gene Williams completed two years of pre-medicine before entering service in June of '43. During operations in Europe, he served as a company aid man in the 71st Infantry Division of the Third U. S. Army. Coming home last April after eighteen months overseas, Yogi soon found he had a "lot in common" with Theta Virginia Tolle. Both live in El Dorado.

Yogi — he had an inspiration.

Although Milton Caniff, well-known creator of "Terry and the Pirates," recently revealed that Virginia Larson, 1946 Jayhawker beauty queen, was his inspiration for Jane Allen, Yogi swears on his honor he had no such inspiration for his Heoweez. For obvious reasons the identity of Gene's model for his fall number pin-up girl on page 52 must remain a staff secret.

After working with him for two years before the war, the Editor was more than happy this fall to welcome Williams back to his old job and appoint him as Art Editor of the 1947 JAYHAWKER.

Gene enjoys his cartooning so much that he's given up medicine for the Fine Arts School and a major in commercial drawing. As you leaf through your annual, you'll know he made a right decision.

The "Yogi" Williams Doc Jayhawk bronze statue.

1964 *Jayhawker M.D.*

1965 *Jayhawker M.D.*

1966 *Jayhawker M.D.*

THE 1946 JAYHAWK

The sixth and final "signature" Jayhawk, known as the "Happy Jayhawk," was drawn in 1946 by journalism student Harold David "Hal" Sandy. Writing on the origins of his Jayhawk in 1971, Sandy noted that Ed Brown, head of KU's public relations, approached him and "suggested that he design a Jayhawk that was not ferocious. Hence the Happy Jayhawk. This bird is an adaptation from all the other Jayhawks." Peace had arrived and the university was looking for a less warlike Jayhawk to represent KU. Like Jayhawk artists before him, Hal printed decals of his mascot, which he sold for ninety-five cents to help fund his college education. He paid twenty-five dollars to copyright the design but allowed the University Bookstore to use his Jayhawk for advertisements. In 1948, he sold the copyright to the bookstore for $250. Years later, Sandy stated that the main purpose for selling his Jayhawk copyright was to help the university to maintain a standard mascot. The University Bookstore got quite a bargain, since the Jayhawk is now worth millions in revenue.

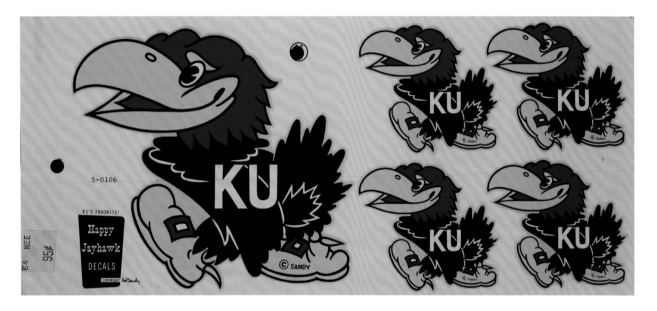

Happy Jayhawk decals with the Sandy copyright symbol.

After his graduation in 1947, with a BS in journalism, Sandy moved to Kansas City and became a marketing consultant. Like George Hollingbery before him, Sandy started his own advertising company, working with such clientele as Coca-Cola, Maytag, and Folgers Coffee. He also participated in a wide variety of civic organizations, serving as an officer and board member of the Kansas City Art Institute, as a founder and board member of the Historic Kansas City Foundation, and two terms as mayor of the city of Westwood Hills, Kansas. He passed away on December 9, 2017, at the age of ninety-three. Sandy's Jayhawk survived for nearly fifty years with no changes until 2005, when the university updated the 1946 Jayhawk.

Throughout the years, many different Jayhawks have appeared on the pages of the Alumni Association's publications. The famous bird is still used today to entertain KU alumni readers and spark memories of their years at school. The mascot strengthens the connection from past to present and speaks a language that all Jayhawk generations understand. The Alumni Association has continued to serve as that bridge, particularly through their development and use of images of the six official generations of the Jayhawk with their dates of creation.

The evolution of the design has been reproduced many times. One of the earliest examples appeared in a brochure published in 1955 by the Student Statewide Activities Association and KU's Alumni Association. It's strange that the date for the Maloy Jayhawk is given as 1908, since Maloy did not arrive on campus until two years later, in 1910. It is also strange that the 1946 Hal Sandy Jayhawk was not included at all. The reverse of the folder introduces what they call "the newest conception of the Kansas Jayhawk." This Jayhawk was created by Roger English, an instructor of design at KU. This "bird winks to show his good nature" but at the same time has a look that is "persistent and determined." This Jayhawk did not really catch on.

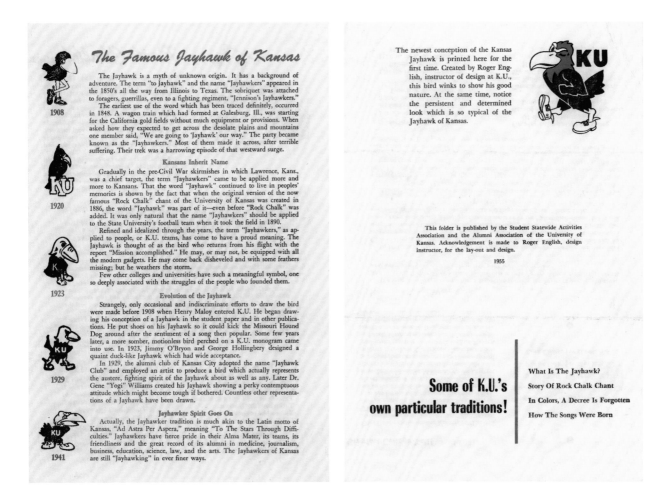

The evolution of the design has been reproduced many times. One of the earliest examples appeared in a brochure published in 1955 by the Student Statewide Activities Association.

One of the Jayhawks that did catch on and now is on display at the center of campus is the "Academic Jay." This prehistoric-looking Jayhawk was cast in bronze by the world-renowned sculptor and KU professor of art Elden Tefft in 1958. The statue, a gift of the class of 1956, is a great place to sit and check your phone or pose in front of for graduation pictures.

Brochure distributed by the Student Statewide Activities Association and the KU Alumni Association, 1955.

The Academic
Jayhawk on Jayhawk
Boulevard.

THE BIBLER AND COKER JAYHAWKS

Despite there being six official Jayhawks, artists continued to make contributions to the Jayhawk record. Between 1947 and 1950, Richard Neal "Dick" Bibler and Paul Alan Coker Jr. drew Jayhawks for the *UDK*, the *Jayhawker*, and the *Sour Owl* and *Bitter Bird*, humorous student magazines. Their Jayhawks were slightly goofy, slightly naughty, and slightly bawdy.

Dick Bibler arrived on campus in the spring of 1946 after serving in the military. Originally from Elkhart, Kansas, Bibler was a consummate businessman, having created his own cartoon production company, Bibler Feature Services, before he'd even arrived on campus. Besides drawing the Jayhawk for various KU publications, he had created a nationally syndicated cartoon called "Little Man on Campus." LMOC, as it was known, was distributed in three different formats: as a single cartoon, as a four-cartoon folded card, and as a small booklet with about twenty pages of cartoons. One could buy the booklet for twenty-five cents at different campus locations.

Above: An original drawing of the Bibler Jayhawk.

Left: The Bibler acknowledgment page from the 1947 *Jayhawker*, 243.

Bibler graduated with a BA in fine arts in 1950 and moved to California. After graduation, he continued to sell his LMOC cartoons to the *UDK* at $4.00 each. He passed away on May 24, 2013, after working as an art professor for thirty years at Monterey Peninsula College.

Paul Coker Jr. was born in Lawrence and enrolled at KU in the fall of 1947 as a fine arts major. He served on the *Jayhawker* art staff and as art editor of the *Bitter Bird* magazine.

Coker was a prolific cartoonist, creating many illustrations for the *Bitter Bird* and the *Jayhawker*. The 1949 yearbook featured his drawing of a "49er" gold miner Jayhawk for the cover art. After graduation in 1951, he continued working as an artist for the Alumni Association through the 1950s, contributing drawings to the *Alumni Magazine* and other

A Paul Coker Jayhawk
from the 1949
Jayhawker, 15.

Paul Coker and
his cartoons were
featured in the 1951
Jayhawker, 228. One
of his Jayhawks can
be seen in the lower
right-hand corner.

alumni-focused projects. In 1961, he began working for *MAD* magazine, eventually illustrating more than 375 articles. Coker also became a production designer on more than a dozen Rankin/Bass television specials including *Frosty the Snowman, Santa Claus Is Comin' to Town,* and *Rudolph's Shiny New Year.* He also drew "Chesty Lion," the official mascot for Lawrence High School.

* * *

In 1966, the university celebrated its centennial. A medallion was struck to commemorate the anniversary and to identify "100 years of outstanding achievements." The December 1965–January 1966 issue of the *Kansas Alumni* magazine included a full description of the medal and its symbols. On the left side is a "textured" column with symbols, including three Jayhawks: "There are three Jayhawks, two at the base of the column and one about a third of the way down from the top of the column. The top bird, following the design of Henry Maloy, c'14, is the earliest of the three. The lowest shows some revolutionary tendency. The bird at the lower left is the latest design; it expresses the fighting spirit of the flock."[4]

In 1990, the Kansas Union began planning for a major renovation. The main entrance received a makeover that included the historic Jayhawks. Just inside the entrance, six four-foot marble and stone inlays of the mascot were set into the floor. This space may be one of the first places that visitors to campus learn about the Jayhawk's evolution over nearly a century.

Above: The University of Kansas Centennial 1866–1966 commemorative medallion.

The floor inlays of the 1912 and the 1923 Jayhawks inside the main entrance to the Memorial Union.

In 2005, the university updated Hal Sandy's "Happy Jayhawk" as part of an effort to strengthen KU's visual identity. The sans serif KU was changed to more closely resemble the Trajan font used in KU's official logo. The long leg on the K is said to represent the hill on KU's campus.

In 2012, KU celebrated the one hundredth birthday of the long-legged Maloy Jayhawk. Since the 1912 Jayhawk had never had a mascot costume, the Alumni Association commissioned one. Named the Centennial Hawk, that Jayhawk was printed on T-shirts and appeared at sporting and other events throughout the year. It now resides in a window display in the Memorial Union bookstore next to the original Baby Jay costume.

An updated 2005 Jayhawk sticker.

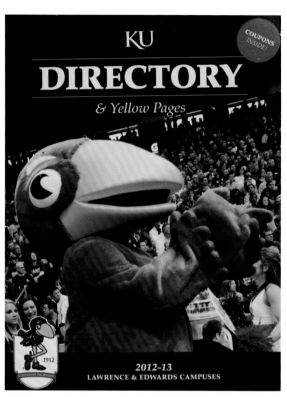

The one hundredth anniversary 1912 Jayhawk appeared on the cover of the 2012–2013 *KU Directory & Yellow Pages*.

A chorus line of Jayhawks from the 1981 *Jayhawker* yearbook, 95.

Images of the evolution of the Jayhawk, dated to mark the passage of time, are used repeatedly to represent the mascot's historical value, linking generations of Kansas alumni. Different entities, including the Office of the Chancellor and the Endowment Association, have used the six Jayhawks on holiday cards and as a promotional device, but the Alumni Association has most often used them to bring together generations of student Jayhawks, as indeed they were the first to publish all the different Jayhawks in one place.

In 1991, the Chancellor Budig family chose these Jayhawks for their "Happy Hawkadays" greeting card.

The changing faces of the Jayhawk as seen through the eyes of journalism students on the cover of the fall 1980 *Jayhawk Journalist*. Note the pencil-beaked Jayhawk in the lower right corner.

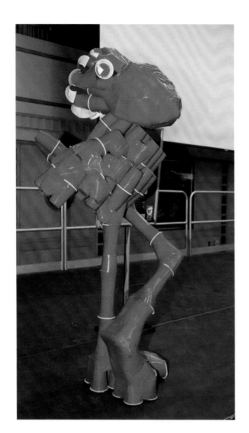

Probably the most bizarre depiction of the Jayhawk evolution came from fine arts student Daniel Scannell. He used red plastic cups to sculpt the birds for his senior project. The sculptures were on display at the Grad Fair in the Kansas Union Ballroom in 2008.

Above: The 1912 Scannell Jayhawk.

Top right: The 1941 Scannell Jayhawk.

Right: Four of Scannell's Jayhawks, the 1912, the 1920, the 1923, and the 1929.

Notes

1. James E. O'Bryon, "The Birth of a Jayhawk," *History of the Jayhawk* scrapbook compiled by Watson Library staff in 1931.
2. Chester K. Shore, "How Did the Jayhawk Get This Way?," *Graduate Magazine*, December 1925, 5.
3. "Offer a New Jayhawk, a Fighting Emblem Is Nominated by K.U. Alumni Here," *Kansas City Times*, October 11, 1929, 2.
4. "The Medal of the Century," *Kansas Alumni* 64, no. 4 (December 1965–January 1966), 11.

3 The Jayhawk as Mascot

The terms "Jayhawk" and "Jayhawker" were in use in Kansas fourteen years before the University of Kansas was established in 1865. Initially, "Jayhawker" did not have a positive connotation, but eventually the term was accepted by the people of Kansas. The transformation of the Jayhawk from its mid-nineteenth-century origins to its ultimate position as the mascot and representative of the University of Kansas was not instant but evolutionary in nature. During the late nineteenth century, the terms "Jayhawk" and "Jayhawker" began to appear more often in university publications, and the Jayhawk started to take on the characteristics of a bird in the early twentieth century.

Mascots are most often aligned with sports teams as good luck charms, but they can also represent businesses that sell products, such as the Pillsbury Doughboy and Tony the Tiger. If the mascot has human characteristics, it's easier and more fun for consumers and fans to relate to the product or the team.

On the field or the court, people in mascot costumes cavort and interact with fans during rallies and sporting events, raising team spirit and spreading joy. Mascots play to the camera and sometimes interact with the opposing team's mascot.

The KU Jayhawk and Kansas State University's Willie the Wildcat in a pregame mock battle, circa 1960.

The Jayhawk became more closely associated with the University of Kansas as the Rock Chalk yell came into use in 1886, and KU sports teams became known as Jayhawkers the following decade. But it's a little-known fact that KU already had a mascot when the Jayhawk took on that role. The first mascot to represent KU at sporting events was also an animal—a bulldog. No documentation exists to explain when or why a bulldog was chosen as KU's mascot, but by the turn of the century, many colleges had live animals as mascots and the bulldog was a common choice. Yale's bulldog, Handsome Dan, is purported to have been the first, in 1890.[1] Drake University in Iowa, Georgetown University in Washington, DC, and the University of Georgia all had—and still have—bulldog mascots. KU Professor E. H. S. Bailey, the man who created the Rock Chalk yell, graduated from Yale, the first university to have a bulldog mascot, so that may have been a contributing factor to KU's decision to adopt a bulldog as its mascot. KU's bulldog, whose name is unknown, was brought to football rallies, games, and parades and can be seen in yearbooks and student scrapbooks.

In this fun image from the 1907 *Jayhawker* yearbook, the bulldog, in his own letter sweater, is shown marching proudly with KU students, 88.

This bulldog symbolizing "that K.U. spirit!" is found in the 1908–1912 scrapbook of KU student Beulah Murphy, 23.

Henry "Hank" Maloy, the creator of the first official Jayhawk, actually drew the bulldog several times. The most notable versions appeared in the 1912 *Jayhawker* yearbook. In "Adventures of the Bull Dog on the Gridiron 1911," Maloy conveys the football season's outcome through a series of imaginative cartoons.

On this page from the 1912 *Jayhawker*, the bulldog is seen as having quite a year on the football gridiron, 472.

Years later, in a letter dated April 26, 1964, Maloy wrote, "It is hard to understand how I could have been drawing cartoons up here for two years without thinking of making a Jayhawk, especially since we had that word jayhawk in the yell all the time. But when I arrived in the fall of 1910 a bulldog was being used as an emblem. It was on pennants, post cards and such things and was being led along in parades at rallies."[2] He went on to write that he didn't like the bulldog, since it was the Yale mascot, so he kept drawing Jayhawks for the *University Daily Kansan*. For a while, the bulldog and the Jayhawk appeared together, as can be seen in this photograph taken in 1917, at the KU–Kansas State Agricultural College football game in Manhattan. Although there are no official KU records regarding the change from the bulldog to the Jayhawk as mascot, the photo below dated 1917 is the last known photo of the bulldog. This suggests that the bulldog was no longer being used as the mascot, particularly since the Jayhawk continued to appear in multiple sources. It is interesting that Maloy asserted he had not seen a Jayhawk for two years, because there are three different Jayhawks in the 1911 *Jayhawker*, the yearbook he worked on as a staff artist.

Bulldog with the Jayhawk at a KU–Kansas State Agricultural College Aggies football game in Manhattan, Kansas, 1917. The Jayhawk wears a sign that says, "I'm the Bird That's Going to Twist That Old Cows Tail."

Over the years, many Jayhawk mascot costumes were created by KU fans, and even by opponents, before the university settled on the official versions. The photo shown below may be the earliest image of a Jayhawk mascot costume. The photo was donated to the University Archives in 2017 by a man who acquired it from an Oklahoma family. The photo was taken at halftime at the Oklahoma–KU football game at Colcord Park in Oklahoma City on November 12, 1910. Kansas won the hard-fought game by a score of 2–0.

In a 1964 letter, Maloy reminisces about another early occurrence of someone wearing a Jayhawk costume. He recalls going to Columbia for the KU–Missouri football game in 1913. The Missourians had a parade the night before the game, and one of the floats was a big cage erected on a hayrack bed with a Jayhawk inside wearing shoes and running back and forth. He declared, "This was the first live Jayhawk I had seen." It is no surprise that Maloy remembered this parade, since he drew a cartoon of the float for the *UDK*.

A person in a Jayhawk costume on the field at the KU–OU football game of November 12, 1910.

Maloy cartoon that appeared in the *University Daily Kansan* after the KU–Missouri game in 1914.

A Jayhawk made an appearance in 1914 on the University of Nebraska football field. This Jayhawk had apparently been stolen from KU at the KU–Nebraska game in Lawrence the year before, on November 15, 1913. After the 1914 game, the *UDK* ran a story "Huskers Produce Stolen Jayhawk," acknowledging that this Jayhawk had been "swiped" by Nebraska the year before and paraded around the field at the next game in Lincoln.

THE KANSAS JAYHAWK.
Later captured and carried off to Lincoln by Nebraskans as a trophy of victory. Funeral rites were observed with due solemnity and ceremony.

Image that appeared in the 1914 Nebraska *Cornhusker* yearbook, 350. Courtesy of Archives & Special Collections, University of Nebraska-Lincoln Libraries.

In 1921, another Jayhawk created by an opposing team made an appearance. Mighty Nebraska was again leading the league in football, and as it happens this was the same game where KU cheerleaders exhorted students to hop in their jalopies and head up to Nebraska to show their team spirit—the same game that spurred O'Bryon and Hollingbery to draw their Jayhawk. A photo montage titled "up in NEBRASKA" that appeared in the 1922 yearbook includes two photos of a very strange-looking bird. In an article published in the *UDK* soon after the game, it was reported, "Between halves a huge black Jayhawker pranced out on the field, and was attacked by an alleged football player who swung a mean battle axe and succeeded in decapitating the Kansas bird. After the death the N.U. rooters pulled that distinctly original burial scene, with the slaw [*sic*] music, mourners and all the rest of the trimmings."

Despite some early attempts at costumes, it wasn't until the 1950s that the KU Alumni Association commissioned the first official mascot costume. The costume was made by the Collegiate Manufacturing Co. of Ames, Iowa, one of the largest distributors of college memorabilia in the United States. The body and head were constructed of chicken wire and covered with blue plush material. The beak and feet were covered with yellow felt, and the eyes, which lit up when KU made a touchdown, were made of plastic dishes. Named Jayhawker, the mascot first appeared on October 3, 1953, at the KU–Iowa State football game. The *University Daily Kansan* reported that "the 'live' replica of KU's mythical bird caused considerable comment. Leading the team on the field at the start of the game, it brought

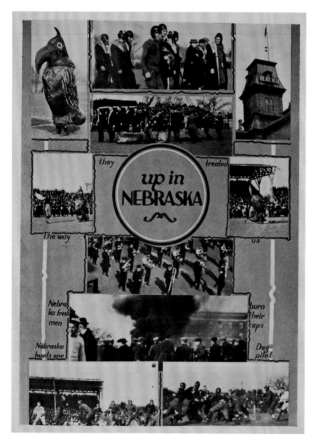

Page from the 1922 *Jayhawker* with scenes from the KU–Nebraska game. Note the two photographs of a very strange Jayhawk in the upper left corner of the page, 133.

Jayhawk mascot and cheerleader on the sideline at the KU–Iowa State football game in Lawrence, October 1, 1953.

'Oh!'s, 'Ah!'s, and 'Isn't he cute?' from the crowd." After that, the Jayhawker began to rou-
tinely appear "in-person" at sporting contests, in photo shoots, at game rallies, and at other
university-sanctioned events.

By the fall of 1958, Dick Wintermotte, assistant secretary of the Alumni Association,
had decided that the first mascot costume, Jayhawk I, needed to be replaced. The Collegiate company couldn't supply another one, so C. E. Tefft, the father of Eldon Tefft, the KU
professor of painting and sculpture who created the large, bronze Jayhawk statue in front
of Strong Hall, helped to build the next one by making the framework out of aluminum
piping. Jayhawk II, as it was called, was of the same design as the first, except taller, at
seven feet.

Each time the costume was remade, it was updated in some way; the shoes, for instance,
changed quite often. The first Jayhawk wore what looks like yellow fabric wrapped around
some kind of a shoe. For a while, cowboy boots dyed yellow were used, then huge yellow
boots made of foam and a vinyl covering worn over an athletic shoe were made. The fabric
that covered the body also changed. During the 1950s and 1960s, the fabric looked like
velvet; later, a heavy felt was used. The shape of the head and beak also changed: for a time
the beak was very narrow, and then eventually it became wider. In the early years, a human
face could be seen behind a screen under the beak. That feature eventually disappeared.

Wearing the costume was a laborious task. It was big, heavy, hot, awkward, and difficult to
see out of. The wearer had to be between 6'1″ and 6'5″ tall and strong enough to carry about

The Jayhawk on the basketball court in 1959. The
face under the very narrow beak can easily be seen.

The Jayhawk at a photoshoot in 1970. The face can still be seen
under the beak, but the head is more substantial.

The top half of the mascot costume being carried at a football game in 1962.

The Jayhawk on a football field wres-
tling with Missouri's Big Tiger and Lil
Tiger mascots in 1962.

fifty pounds for long periods of time. Despite the costume's challenges, the Jayhawk was still
able to act up with opposing team mascots like Missouri's Big Tiger and Lil Tiger.

When the Booth Family Hall of Athletics opened in 2006, a vintage 1960s Jayhawk
mascot costume was installed in a huge glass case. At the front of the case is a caption that
endeavors to explain the dedication of those students who have served as Big Jays.

> HEART OF A JAYHAWK
>
> This Jayhawk costume made its debut in the 1960s. For the men who became Jay,
> putting on the costume was an act of love. Constructed of a steel armature, over-
> laid with chicken wire and dense fabric, the costume was exceedingly heavy and
> hot. Imagine being inside the sweltering 50+-pound costume on a warm football
> Saturday, striding along the sidelines to enthusiastically raise fan support. Rock
> Chalk Jayhawk!

The Jayhawk in the case became famous after carrying a small girl on its tail during halftime at the semifinals of the NCAA basketball championship against UCLA in the spring of
1971. The photo is on display in the Booth Family Hall of Athletics.

In the special Hank Maloy issue of the *Kansas Alumni*, published in November 1971, a
story notes the difficulties involved in transporting the Jayhawk costume: "Several years ago
when the KU basketball team played in the National Invitational Tournament, there were
logistics which had to be resolved in carting the bird from Kansas City to New York. Vince
Bilotta, field director of the Alumni Association, found a solution. He purchased a round-trip
plane ticket for himself and his wife. As one might guess, the Jayhawk rode in the seat next to
Vince, listed on the passenger chart as 'Mrs. Vince Bilotta.'"[3]

Top left: Big Jay showing off an earlier version of himself.

Top right: Big Jay struts along the football field sideline in 1998.

Left: Small girl riding on the Jayhawk's tail, spring 1971.

Bottom left: Big Jay visits with young fans during KU Night at Royals Stadium, July 3, 1980.

A Baby (Jay) Is Born

Baby Jay was the brainchild of Amy Hurst, a sophomore from Madeira, Ohio. In an October 25, 2010, email, Amy shared that when she was a freshman in 1970, she worked at Lum's Restaurant in Lawrence with one of the male students who served as the Jayhawk mascot. She had originally gotten the idea for a baby jay from the car decal with the big Jayhawk and the little Jayhawks following behind. "I bugged him all year about a Baby j. . . . He introduced me to Dick Wintermotte [Alumni Association president] near the end of my freshman year." Wintermotte told Amy that if she built it and they liked it, she could wear it.

She went home to Madeira for the summer and built a Baby Jay costume in the family garage with assistance from her parents and her next-door neighbor.

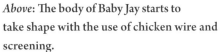

Above: The body of Baby Jay starts to take shape with the use of chicken wire and screening.

Top right: Papier-mâché and blue felt start to define the look of Baby Jay.

Bottom right: A beak is defined . . .

When Amy returned to KU for the fall semester of 1971, she contacted Dick Wintermotte to inform him that she had created a new Jayhawk over the summer. In an October 25, 2010, email, Amy shared that Wintermotte had admitted, "I never thought you'd really do it."

On October 7, 1971, the *University Daily Kansan* ran a story on the festivities planned for homecoming that year. Listed was a performance of the marching band during halftime of the KU–K-State football game and the announcement of "a surprise" feature that would

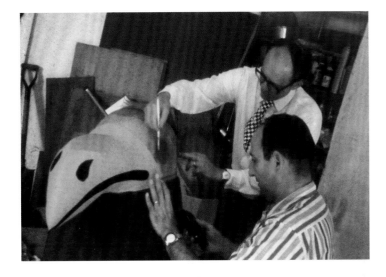

Top left: And eyes start to take shape . . .

Above: Bushy black eyebrows are added . . .

Bottom left: And there you have a Baby Jayhawk. Ready to go to school in the fall.

be added to the program. That "surprise" turned out to be the birth of a new mascot, a baby Jayhawk. While the band played music from *2001: A Space Odyssey* (Richard Strauss's *Also Sprach Zarathustra*), a huge blue egg was pulled toward the center of the field. The egg opened and out came Amy Hurst in the new costume while Big Jay and Chancellor Chalmers waited to greet her. In a November 11, 1983, *UDK* article written by Theresa Quenstedt, Amy remembers, "When I stepped out, you could hear the entire stadium gasping. It was great—quite a thrill." For the first time, the original Jayhawk could be called Big Jay, since there was now a Baby Jay as well.

Later that year, Richard Hurst, Amy's father, officially donated the Baby Jay costume to the university. He noted that the costume had cost $53.94 in materials. In a letter dated December 2, 1971, Irvin E. Youngberg, executive secretary of the University Endowment Association, thanked Hurst for the donation: "The idea certainly has been well received and is an excellent one, creating a further good image of the University of Kansas on so many occasions."

Baby Jay's egg arrives on the football field at the KU–K-State football game.

Baby Jay is helped down from the egg.

Chancellor Laurence Chalmers and Big Jay greet the new mascot.

Eldon Pruett (Big Jay) and Amy Hurst (Baby Jay) pose for the cover of the program for the Kansas–Missouri game, November 20, 1971.

At homecoming in 1972, KU held a major celebration for Baby Jay's first birthday, as reported in the October 30, 1972, issue of *UDK*. During halftime at the KU–Iowa State football game, a huge white "birthday cake" was pulled out onto the field. Jayhawks from 1912, 1929, and 1940 emerged from the side of the cake, and Baby Jay popped out of the top. The band played music appropriate to the era, and the historical Jayhawks rode around the field in a 1926 Model T open roadster, a 1930 Model A touring car, a 1943 Cadillac convertible, and a 1973 Chrysler Imperial.

Big Jay rides on the front of the tractor pulling the giant birthday cake onto the field.

Jayhawks start coming out of the side of the cake, beginning with the 1912 Jayhawk.

Big Jay and the historic Jayhawks gather in front of the cake.

Above and below: When Amy graduated in 1974, a photoshoot was planned to capture her in her Baby Jay costume for a final time.

As with Big Jay, being Baby Jay can be physically demanding. In an October 26, 1976, KU press release, Laddi Snodgrass, who donned the costume for the 1976–1977 school year, described the experience in an interview: "The fiberglass body of the Baby Jay covers the wearer's head and the upper body was built on a framework and weighed about 25 pounds. The framework rests on wooden blocks at the shoulders, and the women wearing the costume must wear regular shoulder pads for protection. My arms and shoulders ached until Wednesday of the next week after each game." Her favorite reason for portraying Baby Jay, though, was the children. They surrounded her at games and asked questions, such as whether she was a real bird.

In September 1978, the unthinkable happened—Baby Jay disappeared! Every two years, the costumes were taken to the Burk Awning & Canvas Goods Manufacturing Co. to be refurbished for the next two years of use. In the September 21 issue of the *UDK*, it was reported that the Baby Jay mascot costume had been taken while sitting on a counter in the store. Robert Burk, an employee of the company, admitted that on September 9, there had been two men in the shop, and when he turned his back they'd picked up the costume and run.

By then, Baby Jay was seven years old, and athletic department officials were determined to keep the tradition of the small mascot alive. The *UDK* story quoted Cathy Stevens, a Salina junior, who had worn the costume for the previous two years, as saying, "There are a lot of people who are very concerned about what happened to the Baby Jay. . . . People who know I do it keep asking me where it is and when it's going to be back. . . . The Big Jayhawk guys miss it terribly. It really made them mad that somebody would go so low as to steal the Baby Jayhawk."

Rather than have another Baby Jay built at a cost of $600, everyone waited to see if she would be returned. After six weeks, a ransom note and photographs were sent to the *University Daily Kansan*. The note was made of cut up letters, and one of the photographs showed the costume with tape over its eyes and beak and its wings tied together. The other photo showed two people in sheets and masks standing over the mascot with a gun and a knife. The note did not ask for a ransom but did say that the bird would be returned.

The Alumni Association and members of two fraternities continued to search for Baby Jay, and messages asking for the mascot's return were flashed on the Memorial Stadium scoreboard during the next three football games.

Finally on October 26, the Thursday night before the KU–ISU homecoming game, an anonymous call came into the *Kansan* telling them that the costume could be found at the top of the Wells Overlook tower about five miles south of Lawrence. A reporter and photographer arrived at the site and found the costume. Law enforcement officers from KU, Lawrence, and Douglas County arrived on the scene a few hours later, and the KU officers took possession of the costume. It was then taken to the Lawrence Police Department to be examined. The costume was intact and not damaged.

Combat with another team's mascot sometimes caused problems. In a humorous story that appeared in the September 1996 issue of the *Kansas Alumni* magazine, Tracee Hamilton, who served as Baby Jay in 1978, confirmed how uncomfortable and immobilizing the Baby Jay costume was, tells a harrowing tale of abuse by Willie Wildcat, K-State's mascot: "Willie had long been known as a vulgar predator in the mascot animal kingdom because he had one distinct advantage—complete mobility. He was basically a 6-foot guy in a fur track suit.

Baby Jay
Paul Schultz, KU police detective, carries Baby Jay down from the top of the observation tower at Wells Overlook, which is about five miles south of Lawrence. The Baby Jay costume was found last night at about 10 p.m. It had been missing since Sept. 9.

Staff photo by RANDY OLSON

Left: The Baby Jay mascot costume found at the top of the Wells Overlook tower and being rescued by Paul Schultz, a KU police detective. *UDK*, October 26, 1978.

Right: The Baby Jay mascot costume waiting to be picked up at the Lawrence Police Department.

No heavy costume. Sneakers not boots. Sure, he had a fiberglass head, but any wimp can wear a fiberglass head. It took a strong yet small woman to wear the whole package." She relates that typically during the K-State game, Big Jay stayed fairly close to prevent Willie from getting up to mischief. But, during one game, she and Big Jay were separated and Willie caught her off-guard. He grabbed her wing and began to swing her around, which caused pain in her arms because of the structure of the suit. Big Jay heard her cries and came to the rescue but not before she sustained bruises that lasted for weeks. Hamilton finishes the story by noting that Baby Jay's costume had changed with the times and was now much more mobile, even allowing Baby Jays to do backflips and somersaults.

Amy Hurst has returned to campus several times for anniversary events. In 2011, she arrived on campus to celebrate the fortieth birthday of Baby Jay. As part of the festivities, her original Baby Jay costume was removed from its storage space in the University Archives in the Kenneth Spencer Research Library and set up in a specially designed display case on the first floor of the student union.

The Kansas Alumni Association keeps the Jayhawk Nation updated about mascot news. On several

This year Baby Jay is head over heels for KU.

Baby Jay flipping on the basketball court, from *Kansas Alumni*, March/April 1992, 9.

57

occasions, Big Jays and Baby Jays have become more than just working partners. At 5:00 am on October 18, 1976, Dave Palenshus and Dede Morozzo, Big Jay and Baby Jay, loaded their bulky costumes in a car and took off for Ames to represent KU at the Iowa State University football game. What started as a friendship turned into romance. In a KU press release titled "Jaybirds Plan to Share Nest," Ms. Morozzo said, "This was the first time we'd really done the Baby Jay and Big Jay thing together. We got to know each other well during that weekend because it was a long one." They announced their engagement the next summer, and the wedding was scheduled for May 1977. Dede and Dave and their guests were surprised when Big Jay and Baby Jay arrived at the wedding reception. Dave and Dede had been succeeded as mascots by two of their friends, who donned the costumes to attend the reception. A second press release concluded, "The supply of napkins on the serving table quickly diminished as the guests appropriated them for autographs. And the bride and bridegroom—they were as happy as their guests to see their feathered friends again. After all, birds of a feather do flock together."

Above: The original Baby Jay costume outside the bookstore in the Memorial Union.

Right: From the September 1977 issue of the *Kansas Alumni*, 10.

Big birds surprise love birds

Unusual guests. Especially at a wedding reception! But, why not? They had come to help celebrate the wedding of their

Christopher Veit and Jessica Virtue also became acquainted while serving as Big Jay and Baby Jay in 2003. They decided to get married several years later and chose October 20, 2008, as the wedding day, "the only stretch during football season with two away games," Virtue explained. "One for the wedding, one for the honeymoon." Plenty of mascots attended the wedding, including the best man and two of the bridesmaids, and the current Big Jay and Baby Jay made an appearance as well.

From the January 2008 issue of *Kansas Alumni*, 8.

Mascot love

When we heard Big Jay and Baby Jay were getting married, we thought it sounded like a marketing idea gone bad. The crazy kids get along so well. Why complicate matters? Turns out we needn't have worried: It's the folks *inside* the suits who are in love.

Christopher Veit, e'05, and Jessica Virtue, c'06, j'06, met while serving on the mascot squad. Being among the select few who fill the big yellow shoes of our feathered icons gave them ample time to get acquainted. A shared passion for all things crimson and blue sealed the deal.

They tied the knot Oct. 20, "the only stretch during football season with two away games," says Virtue. "One for the wedding, one for the honeymoon."

The festivities had a suitably KU flair: The best man and two bridesmaids were former mascots, and Big Jay and Baby Jay made an appearance, too.

"One of the nice things about KU's mascots is we have two, so you can kind of play off each other," says Veit.

Adds Virtue, "It's nice to find someone you can play off so well."

In recent years the Jayhawks have been dressed in different costumes including football and basketball uniforms and tuxedoes for special occasions. The mascots always wear the appropriate uniform for games with Baby Jay as number ½ and Big Jay as number 1. They have appeared as superheroes and have dressed in colorful holiday sweaters. Most recently both mascots marched in the Liberty Bowl parade in Memphis appropriately dressed as Elvis.

From the March 5, 2022, Senior Night against Texas.

Jayhawks in football
and basketball
uniforms.

Above, left and right: Baby Jay as Batman and Big Jay as Robin, January 15, 2017.

Left: The Jayhawks in holiday sweaters, December 8, 2015.

Marching in the
Liberty Bowl parade,
December 27, 2022.

* * *

Once the Jayhawk had been visualized, it took on anthropomorphic characteristics much more easily than mascots of other universities in the Midwest, such as a Nebraska corncob or an Iowa State cyclone. And even among the different Jayhawk manifestations, some are more humanlike than others. Maloy's long-legged Jayhawk is much more human-like and seems to have more personality than any of the other Jayhawks.

As time has passed, the Jayhawk has become woven into all parts of the university, not only athletics. The Jayhawk is not just a mascot; it's a tradition and a true symbol of the University of Kansas. It's hard to imagine KU without the Jayhawk.

Notes

1. Timothy P. Brown, *How Football Became Football: 150 Years of the Game's Evolution* (West Bloomfield, MI: Brown House, 2020), 220–221.
2. Henry Maloy Papers, University Archives, Kenneth Spencer Research Library, University of Kansas.
3. "The Jayhawk and Mr. Maloy," *Kansas Alumni* 70, no. 3 (November 1971): 5.

4 JAYHAWKS IN PRINT

Even though the university has endorsed only six "official" Jayhawks, artists' interest in and reimaginings of the Jayhawk have not diminished. Hundreds of Jayhawks have been used throughout the decades to illustrate newspapers, magazines, and yearbooks, representing a variety of university events, departments, and organizations. These unofficial Jayhawks have been depicted in the *University Daily Kansan*, the KU Alumni Association's *Graduate Magazine* and *Kansas Alumni* magazine, programs for many sporting events, and even the KU phone directory. These and other publications have often featured fun and unique Jayhawks, but the *Jayhawker* yearbook beats them all for sheer volume of its Jayhawks and the creativity of Jayhawk artists. In the words of the class of 1915, the purpose of the *Jayhawker* is to "put the mementos of the past college year into substantial form" so that the class will "be able to recall past memories."

Although the *Jayhawker* yearbooks are gold mines for Jayhawk lovers, the first yearbook to carry the *Jayhawker* title did not feature a single Jayhawk in its pages. The earliest yearbooks were published under a different name each year, such as *Cicala* in 1884, *Helianthus* in 1889, and *Oread* in 1899. In 1901, a committee of student representatives from each class named the university's annual *Jayhawker* in the hope that it would become a permanent

Title page from the 1901 *Jayhawker* yearbook. On the left is a KU graduate with old Blake Hall on the KU campus in the background. On the right is an idealized figure (of a cowboy?) standing on the Kansas prairie. An owl representing wisdom is in the center in an apple tree. Perhaps the tree represents the tree of knowledge? KU student Syd Prentice is the illustrator.

name. That ploy worked. The *Jayhawker* name continued for 110 years, until the last *Jay-hawker* was published in 2011.

Published in 1902, one year after the first *Jayhawker*, *The Jayhawk Quill* was another early university publication to use the term "Jayhawk" in its title. *The Jayhawk Quill* was created by a board of ten students who were interested in producing a literary magazine.

The first KU publication to print an image of the Jayhawk was the 1908 *Jayhawker*. Its drawing of a Jayhawk on a goalpost with the Missouri Tiger below was also the first image of a Jayhawk to be published in the yearbook, as discussed earlier in the chapter on the evolution of the KU mascot. Also in that 1908 yearbook is the cartoon, titled "Tight Wads," of a line of Jayhawks perched on a fence, each smug little bird having a name emblazoned on its beak. "Tight Wads" may refer to those who don't pay for a copy of the yearbook.

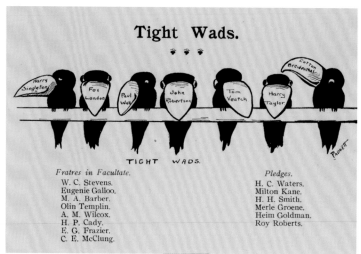

Left: Cover of the *Jayhawk Quill*, March 1902.

Above: "Tight Wads," 1908 *Jayhawker* yearbook.

The 1910 *Jayhawker* featured the next Jayhawk image to appear in the yearbook at the head of a piece called "Jayhawk Talks." This creepy-looking bird somewhat resembles the long-legged Jayhawk that Maloy would draw two years later. Emile Grignard, the yearbook art editor for that year, drew "Mr. Jayhawk" as he endeavors to collect and record stories for his column. He is visited by students and faculty alike in an effort to prevent him from sharing stories and other pieces of gossip. In the piece, he is called "insolent," "Mr. Jaybird," "impertinent," "a warty-little fowl," "conceited," "brainless," and "frivolous," as KU people try to talk to him sensibly about important issues, including student elections and women's suffrage, which he disregards.

In 1912, the first "official" Jayhawk, by Henry "Hank" Maloy, made its appearance. Al-though the *University Daily Kansan*, the student newspaper, can't match the *Jayhawker* yearbook in the number of Jayhawks featured in its pages, it does have the distinction of being the first place that the 1912 Maloy Jayhawk appeared in print.

The 1917 *Jayhawker* was "dedicated to Rock Chalk Jay Hawk K.U." Its pages are decorated with pale blue crow-like Jayhawks with red on their beaks.

Right: 1910 *Jayhawker* yearbook.

Below, left and right: Introductory pages from the 1917 *Jayhawker*.

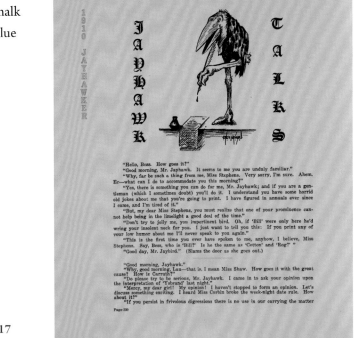

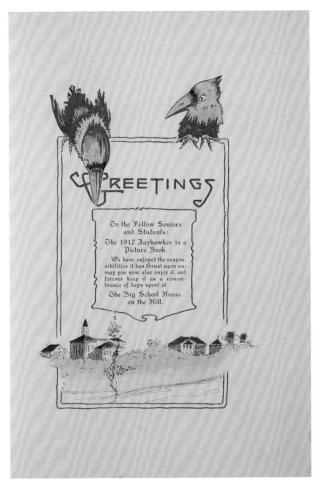

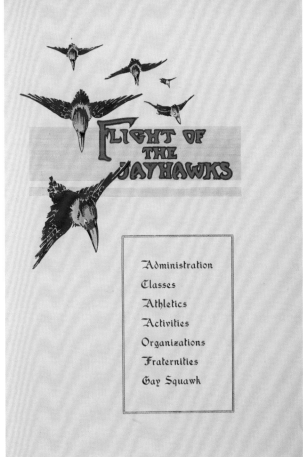

The pastedowns on the inside covers of the 1920 *Jayhawker* depict a flock of Jayhawks flying over a field of sunflowers. A full color drawing graces the beginning of each division of the yearbook, such as Administration and Athletics. In addition, Jayhawks can be found on almost every one of its 448 pages.

The next Jayhawk of note is a morose-looking fellow, perched on a quill pen on the covers of both the 1924 and 1925 yearbooks.

Right: Inside cover of the 1920 *Jayhawker*.

Below left: Page introducing organizations from the 1920 *Jayhawker*.

Below right: The 1924 *Jayhawker*.

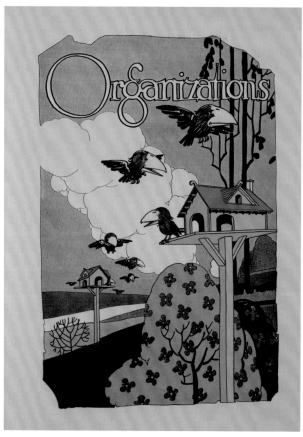

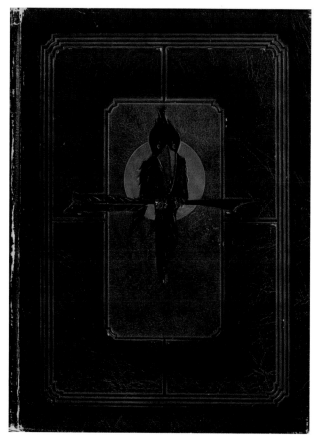

Included in the 1925 *Jayhawker* is a section titled "Hill Life" with photographs of students showing school spirit at rallies and football games, KU buildings in the snow, and student political activities. Running along the top and bottom of these pages is a series of humorous cartoons of the Jayhawk attacking the Missouri Tiger and what may be the wildcat of the Kansas State Agricultural College in Manhattan.

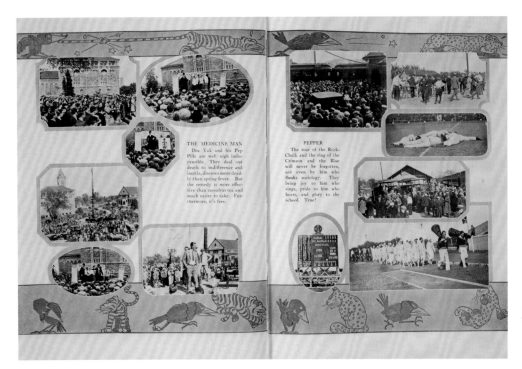

Jayhawk cartoons, 1925 yearbook, 104–105.

The 1928 yearbook has a distinctive Jayhawk on its cover and thirty cute little Jayhawks inside, drawn to match the student activity photos on the page. Sports, including football, basketball, and track; the university concert course; and the opening of the new auditorium (soon to be named Hoch Auditorium) are documented.

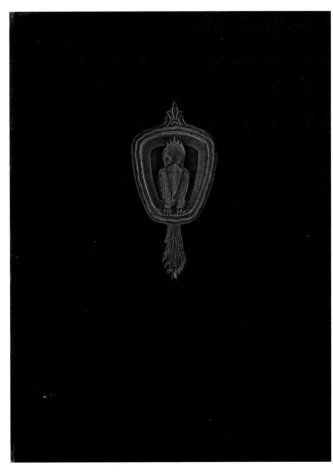

Cover 1928 *Jayhawker.*

The Aggies Are Here

It takes just exactly a special train of Wildcat rooters, a big brass band, a crew of pep hounds—or whatever they call them up the Kaw, and two or three football teams to attract the attention of the proud Jayhawk who is doubly proud after having tasted a football victory or two. People who read the papers, or who were unfortunate to be there, know that the trip was quite a success from the Aggie viewpoint—Oh yes indeed.

A Jayhawk playing football.

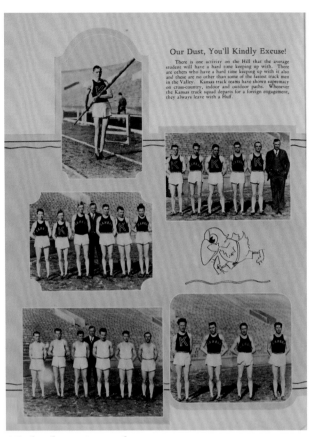

Our Dust, You'll Kindly Excuse!

There is one activity on the Hill that the average student will have a hard time keeping up with. There are others who have a hard time keeping up with it also and these are no other than some of the fastest track men in the Valley. Kansas track teams have shown supremacy on cross-country, indoor and outdoor paths. Whenever the Kansas track squad departs for a foreign engagement, they always leave with a Huff.

A Jayhawk running track.

The University Concert Course

The University Concert Course has offered programs this past season that are unusual both in the talent of the artists and the diversity of attractions. Mme. Amelia Galli-Curci, Albert Spalding, Levinne and Pablo Casals have drawn full houses and have given much toward the satisfaction of music lovers of the University. These artists need no introduction to those familiar with music and but little to any public. Dean D. M. Swarthout of the School of Fine Arts arranged the course.

A Jayhawk singing.

The New Court

This year the Jayhawk found himself on an entirely new vantage point, that was leather cushioned, watching his victorious basketball team smother its foes. The New Auditorium furnished seats to all spectators and the overpacked Robinson Gymnasium was only a memory. But the Rock Chalk thundered just as loud as it did in years past and Missouri Valley basketball and Kansas, its true parent, maintained their supremacy even though Oklahoma chose to accept the Valley title.

A Jayhawk playing basketball.

The 1930 *Jayhawker* is an art deco–styled masterpiece "dedicated to the spirit of youth." A Jayhawk with glowing red eyes appears in the introductory pages, and of special note are the drawings separating the different yearbook sections. These drawings depict the Roman god Mercury with a winged hat and sandals riding a stallion with Jayhawks on the ground below in different poses. These drawings are unattributed.

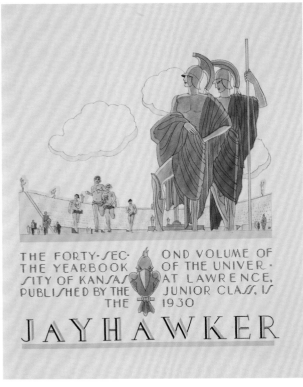

Jayhawks with glowing red eyes can be found on the introductory pages of the 1930 yearbook.

All four classes are shown in this drawing, from the freshman with a beanie to the senior wearing a crown. This page marks the beginning of the "Classes" section of the yearbook.

This image appears at the beginning of the "Limelight" section, which includes campus beauties, the student press, the military, and theatrics, as well as other activities.

A Jayhawk wearing a freshman beanie tries to escape a paddling by Mercury. This drawing introduces the "Organizations" section, including sororities and fraternities.

The cover of the 1931 *Jayhawker* has Jayhawks embossed into the leather of the binding. These birds look quite a bit like robots, and the inside pastedowns are cleverly drawn.

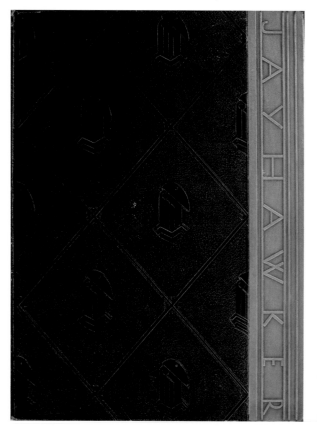

Above, left and right: The 1931 *Jayhawker* cover and inside pastedown.

Right: Close-up of the Jayhawk on the cover of the 1931 *Jayhawker*.

The Jayhawk on the cover of the 1933 yearbook is also art deco in style and shown against a background of geometric shapes. Is he wearing shoes, or are those three little boxes his toes? A similar shoe style, although more extreme, appears on the bird on the cover of the 1935 *Jayhawker*. What is going on with its feet? Are those shoes of some kind? They are certainly different from shoes that had been drawn before and almost look like track shoes or football cleats. The Jayhawk's tail is also a bit strange, looking like it's tucked under the shoes. It may be that this Jayhawk was modeled somewhat after the image that appeared on the 1933 yearbook.

As the years went by, yearbook staffs continued to put interesting Jayhawks on their covers. The cover for the 1941 annual is worth noting. The image is a simple line drawing showing the Jayhawk in silhouette.

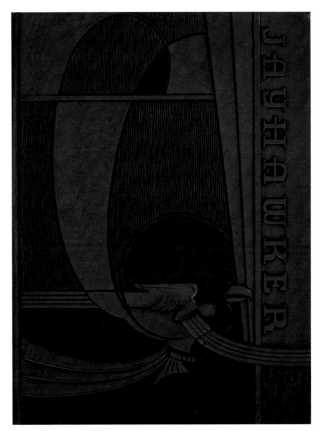

The 1933 *Jayhawker*.

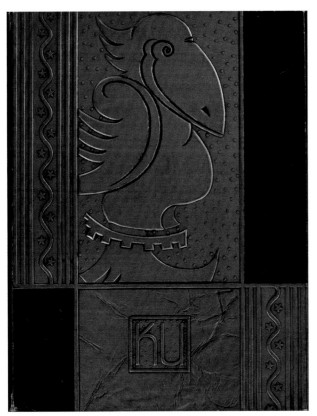

The 1935 *Jayhawker*.

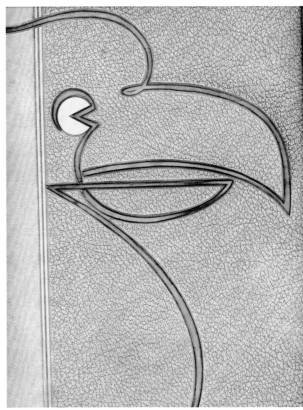

The 1941 *Jayhawker*.

The 1969 *Jayhawker*.

The end of the groovy sixties is capped by the 1969 yearbook. The psychedelic Jayhawk on this cover emerges out of the year, 1969. A beak appears shouting out, "Jayhawker Magazine Yearbook," and the letters K and U make up the eye.

John C. Ritland, art director of the 1974 *Jayhawker*, portrayed the Jayhawk as a businessman, a social worker, a medical doctor and patient, an engineer, and an architect to represent the university's professional schools.

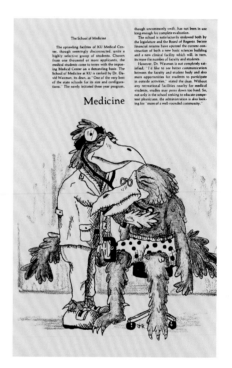

Top left: Ritland's businessman Jayhawk.

Top right: A Jayhawk doctor and patient.

Bottom left: The architect Jayhawk.

Bottom right: Jayhawk representing the Free University.

The 1982 *Jayhawker* celebrates KU traditions and incorporates the six historic Jayhawks to guide the reader through the year. In an introduction to the yearbook, the editors identify the 1912 Jayhawk as a "tradition" that "represents the start of generations of Jayhawks that would pass through the University of Kansas." They conclude, "The bird makes terrific company. Enjoy your trip." The six Jayhawks are skillfully superimposed over line drawings of students, athletes, organizations, and so on that represent the yearbook's sections.

Left: The 1912 Jayhawk at the start of the "Student Life" section.

Bottom left: The 1929 Jayhawk leads the band at the beginning of the "Organizations" section.

Bottom right: All the Jayhawks join in on the "Ads and Index" section.

1993 · JAYHAWKER

UNIVERSITY

June 1925 issue of the
Graduate Magazine.

Next to the *Jayhawker* yearbook, the *Graduate Magazine* (later *Kansas Alumni*), published by the KU Alumni Association to keep alumni informed of university affairs, is probably the publication with the most Jayhawks printed in its pages. An early professorial-looking bird appeared at the head of a column called "Jayhawk Chalk Talks" in the *Graduate Magazine* in the 1920s.

The title banners of the 1931 and 1933 *Graduate Magazine* include two interesting Jayhawks, one spreading its wings over the title and the other seemingly drawn inside a box. As these drawings demonstrate, Jayhawk images were constantly in flux, changing almost from year to year.

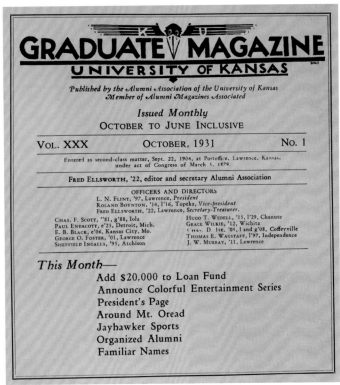

Facing page: Diversity was the theme of the 1993 *Jayhawker*, reflected in its Jayhawks of many colors.

Graduate Magazine, October 1931.

GRADUATE MAGAZINE
UNIVERSITY OF KANSAS

Volume XXXII   DECEMBER, 1933   Number 3

First Turkey Day Homecoming in 10 Years Draws Thousands

GATHERED about the annual Kansas-Missouri game, which is to be played again this year on Thanksgiving Day for the first time in a decade, is a series of events calculated to entertain returning alumni and make them feel that the old school is glad to have them back again. The occasion is called Homecoming. But it can't be Homecoming unless the alumni come home. Every indication a few days before the event showed conclusively that

parade and rally, and mixer at the Union afterward, make it worthwhile to be on hand a day early.

For the first time in history the Homecoming committee this year turned the dance to be held on the eve of the game over to the Student Varsity Dance Committee and permitted a charge to be made. The reception and mixer on the lounge floor of course were to be without charge.

Four hundred and sixty-four second

Graduate Magazine, December 1933.

In the 1920s, athletic programs became popular and sported unique and fun Jayhawks for years to come. Some of the earliest, and most colorful, depictions of Jayhawks are found on the covers of athletic programs for track events and football games.

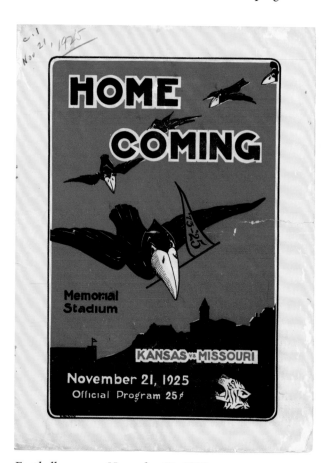

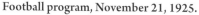

Football program, November 21, 1925.

Kansas Relays program, April 17, 1926.

The *Jayhawk Gridster*, a football magazine, was published through the 1930s with brightly colored Jayhawks on the cover. The 1922 Jayhawk, drawn by O'Bryon and Hollingbery, appeared on a football program from 1933.

Jayhawk Gridster, the KU football magazine, October 22, 1932.

Jayhawk Gridster, October 27, 1934.

Football program, September 20, 1933.

In February 1936, the drawing of a very different-looking
Jayhawk appeared on the cover
of the *Graduate Magazine*. The
new bird, with exotic plumage
on its head and body and a large,
hooked beak, was designed to
celebrate the seventy-fifth anniversary of Kansas's statehood.

After seeing the new Jay-
hawk, Hank Maloy was moved
to write a letter to the *Graduate
Magazine* editors. The letter
was published several months
later, in the November 1936
issue, under the title "Some
Advice from Originator." Maloy
declares that the new Jayhawk "is
going to make plenty of grief for
cartoonists up there [referring
to KU].... Jayhawks, of course,

Cover of *Graduate Magazine*, February 1936.

have moods like the rest of us. And your Jayhawk, for several reasons, can never be made to look other than like a scoundrel."

Included with the letter is a comic strip illustrating some of the many things "that a Jayhawk in everyday use has to do." The Jayhawk in the cartoon is attending a football game against Nebraska, and as the contest proceeds the Jayhawk expresses many emotions through his actions. He is dejected when the Cornhuskers intercept a pass and make a touchdown. He hops with elation when Kansas intercepts a pass and goes ninety yards for a touchdown but cries tears of dejection when an offside penalty for Kansas is declared. This comic demonstrates Maloy's skill as a cartoonist and the fascination the Jayhawk held for him as he revisited drawing the mascot over many decades. With just a few marks of his pen, he's able to change the mood of his Jayhawk.

In 1944, at the height of World War II, another account of the myths that swirled around the Jayhawk appeared in print. *The Mythical Jayhawk*, a lengthy booklet written by Kirke Mechem, secretary of the Kansas State Historical Society, presents a tongue-in-cheek history of the mascot. Mechem claims to be defending the Jayhawk against opposition by Kansas educators who "discovered that one of their own textbooks not only tells little children that it [the Jayhawk] is real but that it is a native of this locality."

Mechem also revisits the purported Irish origin of the word "Jayhawk," as used by Pat Devlin in 1856. He shares that a letter of inquiry was sent to the Library of Dublin asking whether such a bird could be found in Ireland. The responder answered that there "is no such bird in Ireland," but admitted "that the name might exist in an isolated locality for some species." At the end of the letter, the librarian added, "May I suggest that you inquire if history relates whether the original Pat Devlin was known sometimes to have an inventive turn of mind."[1]

THE GRADUATE MAGAZINE

Maloy cartoon, *Graduate Magazine*, November 1936, 7.

Cover of *The Mythical Jayhawk.*

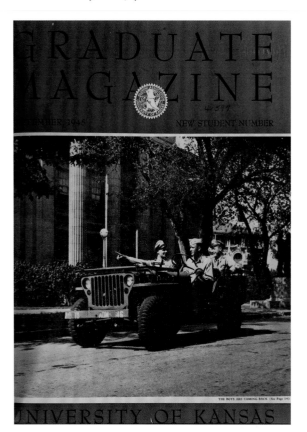

Cover of the September 1945 issue of the *Graduate Magazine.* Note that servicemen are driving down Jayhawk Boulevard in a military jeep.

Irish-born Lawrence resident Reggie Walsh has noted that there is a word in the Irish language, "seabac" (alt. "seabhac"), that when spoken does sound like "jayhawk." Several definitions of "seabhac" appear in Patrick Dineen's classic Irish–English dictionary, including "a hawk or falcon; a hero or champion, a noble man; . . . a sparrow hawk." There is also a phrase using the word that means "when the warriors return raging from battle."[2]

Mechem ends on a patriotic note, proclaiming that "the Jayhawk is peculiarly an expression of the spirit of Kansas. Like the state, it was born in adversity and its flight is to the stars." He goes on to say of the Jayhawk: "Today its free and fierce spirit flies with Kansans on every battle front. . . . Soon the shadow of its wings will fall once more over France." Remember that this book was published during World War II.

In 1956, a slightly revised edition of the original was published with extensive notes that reveal that about a thousand of these pamphlets were sent to Kansans in the armed forces overseas during World War II. The Historical Society also learned that a number of planes, jeeps, tanks, landing craft, and small ships bore the name "Jayhawk" or "Jayhawker."

* * *

In the January 1945 issue of *Graduate Magazine,* a new emblem appeared on the masthead. This global Jayhawk, used for the rest of the decade, was in recognition of the worldwide influence of KU graduates.

During the war years, the Alumni Association sought to identify and communicate with Jayhawks in the service. A feature in the *Graduate Magazine* titled "In Defense of the Nation" presented two Jayhawks in military uniform and shared news about those in service, including the date they graduated from KU, what branch they were serving in, and their location.

* * *

An unknown Jayhawk artist chronicled the 1946 football season by creating a series of eleven small cards, with a new one printed for each game. Each card included a cartoon of the Jayhawk overcoming the opposing team's mascot, as well as a quote from KU's football coach, George Sauer.

LYLE ARMEL, '20, has won promotion to the rank of Lieutenant Commander in the Navy. He held that rank as a reserve officer but was called back into service last July as a Lieutenant. He enlisted in the Navy in 1917 and rose to the rank of Lieutenant in World War I. By continued training he acquired twenty-one years of service in the naval reserves. Lieut. Commander Armel is gunnery officer on the transport St. Mihiel operating in the Pacific. He also has other duties such as morale officer and member of various important committees. Mrs.

Jayhawks in military uniforms on the "For the Defense of the Nation" feature in the March-April 1942 *Graduate Magazine*, 11.

The Jayhawk skins the Kansas State Wildcats.

The Jayhawk rides an Iowa State Cyclone.

The Jayhawk attacks Denver University's Pioneer Pete.

The web-footed Jayhawk from the *Kansas Historical Quarterly*, republished in the *Graduate Magazine*, October 1947, 17.

A web-footed Jayhawk graced the October 1947 issue of the *Graduate Magazine*. Originally published in the *Kansas Historical Quarterly*, the story of this Jayhawk was shared in a letter from Lt. Colonel Lowell R. Whitla, who graduated from KU in 1920. This Jayhawk, based on the 1929 version, was painted on the forward port and the starboard sides of his ship the USS *Radon*. (After further research, a USS *Raton* was identified but not a USS *Radon*.) He writes, "They [the Jayhawks] were eight feet high and wore the crimson and blue colors of a true Kansan. Now this particular Jayhawk was one of the old timers and no longer a college boy. So, in place of the letters "K" and "U," he carried an ordnance bomb under one wing and a very serviceable monkey-wrench under his other wing. . . . This seagoing bird of warlike demeanor is in sharp contrast to the peacetime Jayhawk of the 'huggin' and a chalkin' era."

The KU telephone directory began to include Jayhawks on its cover in the 1937 academic year. In later years, both Yogi Williams and Dick Bibler contributed drawings for the directory.

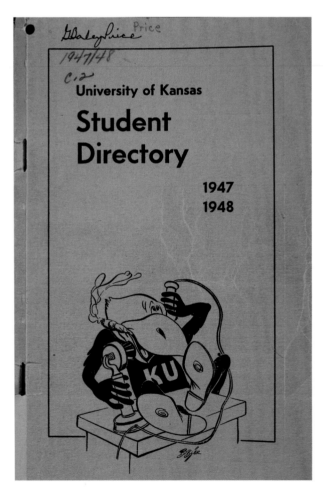

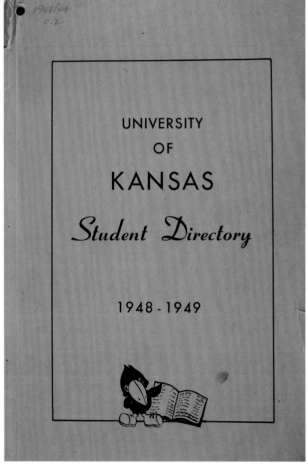

Dick Bibler drew one of his Jayhawks for the cover of the student directory of 1947–1948, and a cute bird appears on the cover of the 1948–1949 directory.

In 1940, a colorful academic Jayhawk appeared on the invitation for the annual commencement luncheon, and in 1949, the Home Economics Department at KU began using a "Coed Jayhawker," designed by Mrs. Doris Wilcox, as their mascot.

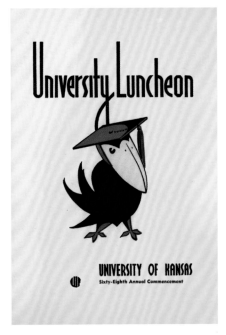

Invitation to the University Luncheon, Commencement, 1940.

Coed Jayhawker of 1949.

In the spring of 1966, the School of Journalism began publishing their newsletter, the *JayHawk Journalist*, using a tough Jayhawk reporter with a press pass in his hat and a pen and pad for taking notes.

Fall 1971 issue of the *JayHawk Journalist*.

1965–1966 Annual Report of the Firemanship Training Program of KU's Extension Service.

Since 1927, the statewide Firemanship Training Program has worked in partnership with the University of Kansas Extension Service, and several different Jayhawk designs have represented the program. The first design of a Jayhawk fireman zooming around on a fire extinguisher dates to 1965–1966.

The G-Hawk was originally drawn by Raymond C. Moore, University Distinguished Professor of Geology. In the late 1960s, Roger Williams designed the cover of the *G-Hawker* or *Geology-Hawker* by adapting Moore's Jayhawk. The G-Hawk is resting his booted foot on Lindley Hall, where the Department of Geology is located.

The Jayhawk on this poster from September 1974 is the perfect symbol for a group that is interested in Kansas birds and birding. Now, that Jayhawk really does look like a jay!

Cover of the Spring 1974 issue of the *G-Hawker*.

Notice of the September 19, 1974, Jayhawk Audubon Society meeting.

Many of the programs for the Kansas Relays included imaginative Jayhawks on their covers. Two examples of these intense Jayhawks were drawn as participants in the Kansas Relays for the 1988 and 1995 seasons. These Jayhawks look like they have super skills!

63 YEARS AND RUNNING!

Kansas Memorial Stadium
Jim Hershberger Track
April 20-23, 1988

Program for the sixty-third annual Kansas Relays, 1988.

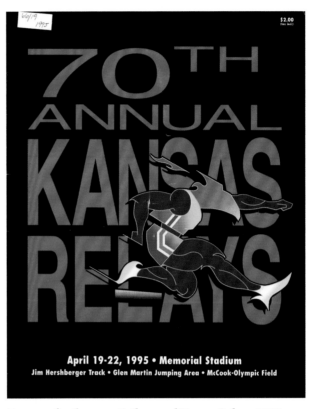

Program for the seventieth annual Kansas Relays, 1995.

During the 1980s, Watkins Health Center incorporated the Jayhawk's beak in an imaginative campaign to catch the attention of students. The catch phrase "Be*ak* Healthy" is still used by Watkins today, including in its work during the COVID-19 pandemic.

During the years 1971–1974, 1983–1986, 1994–1995, and 2010–2011, small Jayhawk cartoons were used in the *University Daily Kansan* to convey weather information to students. The early history of Weather Jay is traced in a piece written by Chris Lazzarino for the *Kansas Alumni* magazine in 2001. *UDK* staff cartoonist David Sokoloff drew the first Weather Jay in 1971; a different bird appeared in the 1980s, drawn by Kelly Green, and was followed by the 1990s weather bird, drawn by art designer Noah Musser. Musser wanted to resurrect Sokoloff's Jayhawk and diligently searched earlier issues of the *UDK* for Sokoloff's design to use as a model. In 2007, Weather Jay reappeared and underwent another change between 2010 and the spring semester of 2011.

BEAK HEALTHY newsletter from the Watkins Health Center, Fall 1991.

Top left: The first Weather Jay appeared in January 1971.

Top center: The Weather Jay of March 18, 1986.

Top right: The Weather Jay of May 10, 2011.

Second row: Noah Musser's Weather Jay, October 31, 1994.

Third row: "What's the Weather, Jay?" feature appeared in January 2013, 2a.

Bottom: The "Campus Chirps Back" question on January 31, 2013, 7a.

Also at that time, a new type of Jayhawk appeared in the *UDK* in a feature titled "Campus Chirps Back." The new bird, which was cute, round, and reminiscent of Baby Jay, brought the Jayhawk into the twenty-first century. Students were invited to connect to the *UDK*'s Twitter account to respond to a daily question. One of the Tweets submitted would be posted in the newspaper the next day.

The University of Kansas Endowment Association has been assisting the university since its charter by the State of Kansas in 1893. In the 1990s, they began using a unique, stylized Jayhawk as part of their logo—demonstrating that all you need is a red dot and two swoops to create a Jayhawk. They also incorporate Jayhawks in their engagement mailings such as this calendar for 2021.

Logo of the University of Kansas Endowment Association.

KU Endowment Association promotional calendar, 2021.

Recent artists in the *Kansas Alumni* magazine have created colorful Jayhawks that look nothing like their Jayhawk ancestors. Larry Leroy Pearson drew for the magazine in the later part of the twentieth century and into the beginning of the twenty-first.

Many of Pearson's most enjoyable drawings appear as illustrations in *The Three Little Jayhawks,* a children's book published by the association in 2007.

The Jayhawk as football coach outlining plays in the volume 95, number 3, 1997 issue of the *Kansas Alumni* magazine, drawn by Larry Leroy Pearson, 9.

But can they talk the talk?

The Three Little Jayhawks as told by Football Coach Don Fambrough and published by the Kansas Alumni Association in 2007.

88

Charlie Podrebarac, who graduated from KU in 1981, has contributed illustrations for features, cover stories, and most often the Jayhawk Walk department of the magazine. Charlie drew for the magazine from the late 1980s into the early 2000s.

Charlie Podrebarac drew this crazy Jayhawk for the "Jayhawk Walk" department of *Kansas Alumni* for the volume 106, 2008, issue.

"Jazz Showdown" illustration drawn by Charlie Podrebarac for the February 2014 issue of *Kansas Alumni*.

Besides *The Three Little Jayhawks*, many other Jayhawk-themed children's books have been published within the past twenty-five years. One example is *The Big Blue Eggventure: The Hatching of Baby Jay*. This fun book was published in 1997 and was authored by Deeann Downs and Jennifer Embrey Orth, with illustrations by Katherine Trueman-Gardner.

The Big Blue Eggventure: The Hatching of Baby Jay, published by Anchor Press, 1997.

Notes

1. Kirke Mechem, *The Mythical Jayhawk* (Topeka: Kansas State Historical Society, 1944), 3.
2. Patrick S. Dinneen, *An Irish-English Dictionary* (Dublin: Education Company of Ireland, 1927).

5 JAYHAWKS AND STUDENT LIFE

No school would exist without its students. And while the purpose of attending a college or university is to acquire an advanced education, other experiences color student life as well. At KU, there has always been a close relationship between the Jayhawk and the student body. The evidence of this relationship is everywhere—in athletic programs, on homecoming parade floats, in student scrapbooks, on class banners, and on T-shirts. Many traditions have come and gone over the long history of KU, but the Jayhawk has been carried on the shoulders of thousands of KU students continuously from one decade, one generation, to the next.

Although the Jayhawk has been drawn in many different ways through the years, he is as easily recognized in the 1990s as he was in the 1930s. The Jayhawk remains a strong and beloved symbol that provides multiple generations of students, past and present, with a shared sense of community.

Underpinning the special relationship between the Jayhawk and KU students are the twin facts that almost all Jayhawks have been created by and for students and that the mascots themselves are students. Whether crowd-surfing at a football game, leading cheers, or lending its image to multiple publications, the Jayhawk is often at the heart of student activities.

The *Jayhawker* staff for the 1954 yearbook felt the pressure that came with being guardians of the Jayhawk. The fall issue begins with a joint statement: "A Jayhawker is a mythical bird, adopted as a symbol to represent the spirit of the people of Kansas: pleasant but not shallow, industrious but not grasping, proud but not arrogant. All this lies behind the name of this magazine-annual published by and for the students of the University of Kansas. It's a demanding heritage."

A Jayhawker is a mythical bird, adopted as a symbol to represent the spirit of the people of Kansas: pleasant but not shallow, industrious but not grasping, proud but not arrogant. All this lies behind the name of this magazine-annual published by and for the students of the University of Kansas. It's a demanding heritage.

Introductory page from the 1954 *Jayhawker.*

Big Jay surfing the crowd at a KU home-coming football game, October 13, 2004.

Keeping a scrapbook of one's college memories was very popular from the late nineteenth century through the first half of the twentieth century. As a device for personal storytelling, students pasted on the album's craft paper pages all manner of memorabilia related to their activities at KU. Photographs, sporting event and theater programs, movie tickets, dance cards with tiny pencils on a string, pieces of ribbon and fabric snipped from a favorite dress, and even candles and matchbooks were pasted into the books. The specially designed KU scrapbook with a large red K on the blue cover was available to students in the college book-store. Here are examples of student scrapbooks that included Jayhawks on their pages.

Opening memory book page from the scrapbook of Catharine Van Keuren, 1918–1924, with ribbons in the appropriate crimson and blue colors.

92

Top left: Photograph of students sharing a KU scrapbook from the Eileen Burkhart scrapbook, 1911–1915.

Top right: An early postcard dated 1910 of the Jayhawk twisting the tail of the Missouri Tiger from the scrapbook of Beulah Murphy, 1908–1912.

Middle: Page from the scrapbook of Emery McIntyre, 1916, 43. Note the KU scrapbook drawn into the picture and Maloy's Jinx character.

Bottom: Page from the Aeo Hill scrapbook, volume 2, 1919–1921. Aeo pasted a candle with KU ribbons into her scrapbook.

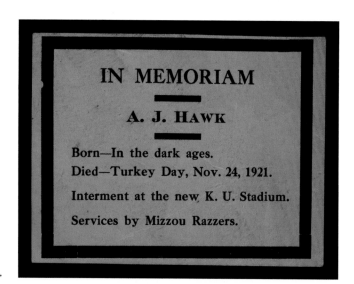

A small card, most
likely created by
Missouri, from the
Aeo Hill scrapbook,
volume 2, 1919–1921.

Page from the Janet
Wilkerson scrapbook,
1937–1938.

Facing page: Page
from the Mary Helen
(Harper) Powers
scrapbook, 1946–
1948 with ticket
stubs and a Jayhawk
matchbook.

Closing Hours Set For Final Week

Closing hours for women during final week and the period between semesters have been announced by the dean of women.

The hours will be 11 p.m. on Wednesday, Thursday, and Friday; 12:30 a.m. Saturday; and 11 p.m. on Sunday, Monday, Tuesday, day, and Feb. 5.

During the period between semesters Feb. 6 through Feb. 12, closing hours will be 12 p.m.

Pi K A Pledges Two

Pi Kappa Alpha announces the pledging of Jack Bryant, engineering freshman of Kansas City, and Billy L. Robertson, business junior, of Peru.

* * *

UNIVERSITY OF KANSAS
LAWRENCE, KANSAS

STUDENT
UNION
BOOK
STORE

Compliments of

KU

Close Cover Before Striking

GAME
3

January 24, 1947 -:- 7:30 P. M.
IOWA STATE COLLEGE
— VS —
KANSAS UNIVERSITY
NOT GOOD IF DETACHED

ary 15, 1947 -:- 7:30 P. M.
RASKA UNIVERSITY
— VS —
ISAS UNIVERSITY
GOOD IF DETACHED

728433
JAYHAWKER
THEATRE

F. Tax .41
Total 49c
724275

THEY'LL ADD WEIGHT
Texas Christian university can toss 664
the University of Kansas Jayhawkers wh
8 o'clock Saturday night in Blues stadium
Meyer's none-too-gentle forward-wall te
Kilman, 205, end; Weldon Edwards, 215
224, guard.

STU
BOO
Memori
Univer
Clerk Amo
E   -0.

JAN 14

SHARE TH
This recei
redeemabl
of its fac

THIS BOOK IS NOT
TRANSFERABLE
THIS IS TO C
Mary
Is a Member of the
UNIVERSIT
SPRING SEME
and is entitled to admission to a
term, subject to condition
$5.50 (plus Fed. tax

Thank You!

95

Homecoming at KU has been an important school tradition for more than one hundred years. The first homecoming in America—which would serve as the model for the college traditions of the big football game, parade, and spirit rally with a bonfire—is said to have been held at the University of Missouri in 1911. Other schools held homecoming-like events several years earlier, including Baylor University, in 1909, and Southwestern University in Georgetown, Texas, in 1909. That first homecoming football game held on the campus of the University of Missouri was against the Kansas Jayhawkers. The game ended in an unsatisfactory tie, 3–3.

Above: A large rally with students circling the bonfire circa 1910.

Facing page: Apparently a charge of dynamite was used to send the Missouri Tiger "to eternity" at that first victorious homecoming in 1912. Maloy's Jayhawk made it onto this page from the 1913 *Jayhawker* along with a beat-up and bandaged Tiger, 136.

The next year, on November 23, 1912, KU reciprocated by holding its first homecoming. The invitation to alumni to visit their alma mater appeared on the front cover of the *Graduate Magazine* of October 1912: "The first 'Homecoming' at the University of Kansas will be celebrated November 23, the day of the Missouri game. Put that in your datebook now. You're expected."

On the Friday night before that first homecoming football game, KU students celebrated their team spirit by building a tower of wood on which to burn a wooden effigy of a tiger. KU students have a long history of building bonfires, likely dating to the 1890s. Wooden crates, old furniture, and anything else made of wood was tossed on top and set on fire to ignite student spirit before a big game. Most years, Missouri served as the opponent at KU homecoming, but on alternating years KU hosted another conference team, such as the Nebraska Cornhuskers or the Iowa State Cyclones. Once homecoming was established as an annual event, student rallies around bonfires were included in the festivities. The exact date of the last bonfire is uncertain, but it may have occurred in 1966.

WHO SAID OUR GIRLS LACKED SPIRIT?

WHO'S WINNING? SEE HAMILTON'S FACE

CON SQUIRES

DIDN'T HE WEEP
DIDN'T HE WAIL?

RED LUPTON
MASCOT

THE TIGER BAND

HIS PITIFUL WAILS HAD NO EFFECT ON THE MOB.

AND IN A MOMENT A CHARGE OF DYNAMITE
SENT HIM TO ETERNITY.

98

Beginning in the early 1920s, students decorated their residences with signs and displays exhorting the football team to win and welcoming alumni back to campus. This activity became an important part of the homecoming festivities, and over time the displays have become more intricate and elaborate, with many including moving parts. In the 1930s, parades with floats became popular. A Jayhawk battering the opposing team's mascot was often the theme of the tableaus.

Facing page: Building bonfires and burning the Missouri Tiger in effigy was a popular activity in the early years at KU. In 1913, the Jayhawkers lost to the Tigers in Columbia, so the Jayhawk is wearing a bandage over one eye, 1914 *Jayhawker*, 196.

The Beta Theta Pi house decorated for homecoming, 1935. A fierce-looking Jayhawk is carrying a Nebraska corncob in its beak and another Jayhawk (*right front*) looks like it's building a nest on a corn shock.

In 1938, these students worked on a float for the home-coming parade. KU played the Nebraska Cornhuskers that year.

Since 1956 most homecomings have been themed, and many of those themes were designed around the Jayhawk. In 1975, the theme was "Jayhawk Rebellion," and in 1996, it was "Jayhawk for President." "Once a Jayhawk, Always a Jayhawk" was the theme in 2006, and that year sidewalk art played a part in the celebration.

Right: Students setting up decorations with an unusual-looking Jayhawk in front of a residence hall for homecoming 1975. That year, the theme was "Jayhawk Rebellion."

Below: The Jayhawk and the Missouri Tiger are caged with each other on this 1983 homecoming float (reminiscent of the 1914 drawing by Hank Maloy). The theme that year was "Under the Big Top."

The theme for this float in 1996 was "Jayhawk for President."

The homecoming theme in 2006—"Once a Jayhawk, Always a Jayhawk"—spelled out in sidewalk chalk and cans, from the 2007 *Jayhawker*, 156.

Many students enjoy being in the crowded stands and next to the basketball court, and their attendance at sporting events is important for school spirit. Through the decades, Jayhawk fans have worn a variety of pieces of headwear to convey their school spirit while attending sporting events, including beak sun visors, Jayhawk hats of different varieties, and even glasses with beaks.

Jayhawk beak sun visors were distributed to the crowd before this football game in the 1950s.

Two alumni in Jayhawk hats at the KU football game on October 8, 1976.

KU fans wearing Jayhawk beak glasses at the KU–K-State basketball game in Dallas in 1989.

Three KU football fans in Hawk hats at the KU–K-State game on October 7, 2000.

The anthropomorphic qualities of the Jayhawk provide opportunities for students to model the mascot after a person, such as the football player in this illustration from the yearbook. One wonders, were the students turning themselves into Jayhawks or turning Jayhawks into students?

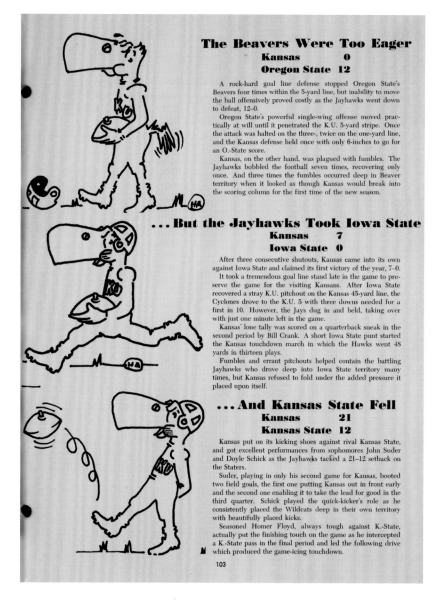

The Beavers Were Too Eager
Kansas   0
Oregon State 12

A rock-hard goal line defense stopped Oregon State's Beavers four times within the 5-yard line, but inability to move the ball offensively proved costly as the Jayhawks went down to defeat, 12–0.

Oregon State's powerful single-wing offense moved practically at will until it penetrated the K.U. 5-yard stripe. Once the attack was halted on the three-, twice on the one-yard line, and the Kansas defense held once with only 6-inches to go for an O.-State score.

Kansas, on the other hand, was plagued with fumbles. The Jayhawks bobbled the football seven times, recovering only once. And three times the fumbles occurred deep in Beaver territory when it looked as though Kansas would break into the scoring column for the first time of the new season.

...But the Jayhawks Took Iowa State
Kansas   7
Iowa State 0

After three consecutive shutouts, Kansas came into its own against Iowa State and claimed its first victory of the year, 7–0.

It took a tremendous goal line stand late in the game to preserve the game for the visiting Kansans. After Iowa State recovered a stray K.U. pitchout on the Kansas 45-yard line, the Cyclones drove to the K.U. 5 with three downs needed for a first in 10. However, the Jays dug in and held, taking over with just one minute left in the game.

Kansas' lone tally was scored on a quarterback sneak in the second period by Bill Crank. A short Iowa State punt started the Kansas touchdown march in which the Hawks went 48 yards in thirteen plays.

Fumbles and errant pitchouts helped contain the battling Jayhawks who drove deep into Iowa State territory many times, but Kansas refused to fold under the added pressure it placed upon itself.

...And Kansas State Fell
Kansas   21
Kansas State 12

Kansas put on its kicking shoes against rival Kansas State, and got excellent performances from sophomores John Suder and Doyle Schick as the Jayhawks tacked a 21–12 setback on the Staters.

Suder, playing in only his second game for Kansas, booted two field goals, the first one putting Kansas out in front early and the second one enabling it to take the lead for good in the third quarter. Schick played the quick-kicker's role as he consistently placed the Wildcats deep in their own territory with beautifully placed kicks.

Seasoned Homer Floyd, always tough against K.-State, actually put the finishing touch on the game as he intercepted a K.-State pass in the final period and led the following drive which produced the game-icing touchdown.

103

1959 *Jayhawker* yearbook, 103.

In the November 1943 issue of the *Jayhawker*, a Jayhawk represented both Joe College and a student who had enlisted in the US Navy and the army for a piece titled "The old order changeth—And here's the new." Campus was changing because of the war, and if you were an enlisted man, your time was not always your own. There was no more sitting at the soda fountain at the Union until late, because popping out of bed at 6:00 am with a "Yes sir!" was required. And there was no more breakfast, lunch, or dinner—it was all simply "chow"! In the beginning, a gap existed between the two types of college life experienced by enlisted and non-enlisted students, but after several months' time, the gap disappeared. The *Jayhawker* reported, "The army, the navy and the civilians have combined forces. They have become a student body and K.U. has again become a college."

Yearbook staff member Mary Olive Marshall drew this Jayhawk wearing black-and-white oxfords and smoking a pipe like a regular "Joe College," but also wearing a military uniform with a navy cap like an enlisted man, November 1943 *Jayhawker*, 12.

Cartoon by Marshall

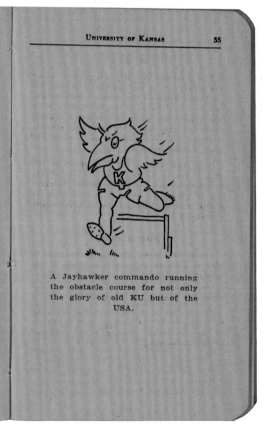

INTRAMURALS

Under the direction of Forrest C. Allen, KU's basketball coach, the intramural program for this year will concern itself primarily with the war effort.

Because the country needs physically fit men for its army and navy, and because too many young men are being rejected on the basis of their physical unfitness, the 1943-1944 intramurals setup will stress aquatics, gymnastics, combative activities, and sports and games in a four-point program.

Since basketball is placed on the number one list of activities for getting men into good physical condition, it will have considerable importance placed upon it. And since men must cross the sea to fight, it is necessary that they be proficient swimmers.

In all phases of combat, on land or sea, the young man trained in the KU intramural program will have the advantage, for during his training at the University, he will not only be taught combative activities with which to overcome the enemy, but he will be in the best physical condition that a daily program of gymnastics, sports, games, and aquatics can make him. It is to produce the physically competent soldier that the intramural program is designed.

A Jayhawker commando running the obstacle course for not only the glory of old KU but of the USA.

The *K-Book* of 1943–1944 with the "Jayhawker commando" leaping over an obstacle in his path.

The *Students' Handbook*, or *The K-Book* as it became known, was originally published by the Young Men's and Young Women's Christian Associations. First released in 1891, the pocket-sized book included all the information a new KU student would need. Sports schedules, railway timetables, location and denominations of churches and religious organizations, advertisements for Lawrence businesses, a campus map, a list of things a freshman woman should know, information about student organizations, fraternities, and sororities, and of course the lyrics to the "Crimson and the Blue" and the Rock Chalk yell all appeared in the handbook.

The *K-Books* didn't include many Jayhawk images, but some are worth noting. Familiar Jayhawk artists, including Yogi Williams, Dick Bibler, and Paul Coker, drew illustrations for *K-Book* covers during the 1940s and 1950s.

In the student handbook of 1943, for example, a drawing of a "Jayhawker commando" running an obstacle course was used to inform students about basketball coach Forrest "Phog" Allen's physical fitness program, which would "concern itself primarily with the war effort." The intramural program promised to provide young men with the opportunity to learn "combative activities with which to overcome the enemy" and to train them to be in excellent physical condition.

The *Sour Owl*, a humorous literary student magazine published between 1914 and 1956, also didn't have many Jayhawks on its pages, but a few are notable. A truly funny Jayhawk and Missouri Tiger with big grins appeared in a two-page spread in the November 30, 1916, issue. The two mascots are encircled by a tiger's tail with knots representing Kansas triumphs.

A "Yogi" Williams family decorates the cover of the 1947–1948 K-Book.

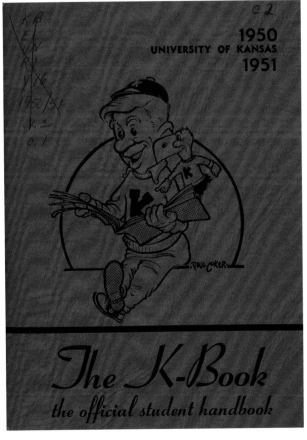

Paul Coker drew this very helpful little Jayhawk perched on the shoulder of a new student in 1950.

Below is a cartoon of the Jayhawk pulling on the Tiger's tail, with small Jayhawks sitting on a fence representing the student cheering section known as the "thundering thousand." Benjamin Minturn, the *Sour Owl* art editor, drew these Jayhawks as a "Fanciful Foolishness for Football Fans."

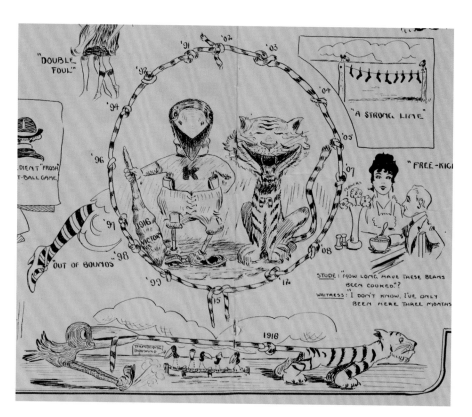

Right: The *Sour Owl*, November 30, 1916.

Above: November 1927 *Sour Owl* cartoon with a Jayhawk in a football helmet and a very creative-looking Missouri Tiger.

Right: Cover of the May 1930 issue of the *Sour Owl*.

A very imaginative MU Tiger and Jayhawk cartoon, drawn by Robert Baughman, made it into the November 1927 issue of the *Sour Owl*. The colorful drawing on the cover of the "Bye-Bye" number of the *Sour Owl* was created by Carl A. "Posty" Postlethwaite. School is over in this May 1930 issue, and two sweethearts are saying goodbye. They are ringed by three little Jayhawks that look like a traveler, a vagabond, and a train porter.

In the 1920s, a Jayhawk cleverly constructed with paper clips, an ink bottle, and a pair of scissors was created to represent the KU Press Club.

Like mascots, pep clubs and cheerleaders are important elements for rousing team spirit both before and during games. The women's pep club, the Jay Janes, began in early 1923. They wore all white, including white stockings, caps, and a sweater with an unusual patch in which the Jayhawk resembles a thunderbird with wings outstretched.

The Red Peppers, a freshman women's pep club, started in the mid-1930s and changed their name to the Frosh Hawks in 1960. The Frosh Hawks wore a large patch with a Jayhawk on their uniforms. The group disbanded sometime during the 1968–1969 school year.

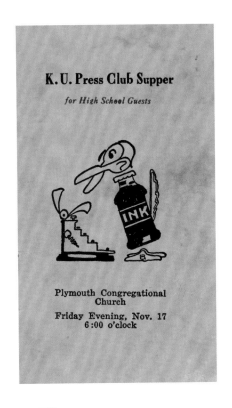

Above: Invitation to the KU Press Club Supper for High School Guests from the Lela Duncan Cardoza scrapbook, November 17, 1922.

Left: In the early years, the pep club was known for its member formations on the football field during halftime, circa 1922.

Left: Jay Janes, women's pep club, 1927.

Above: Patch of the Frosh Hawks, the freshman women's pep club.

Twente Hall, now home to the School of Social Welfare, was originally built to serve as the student hospital with funds donated by Elizabeth M. Watkins. When Watkins Memorial Hospital opened in 1932, the rooms and furnishings were decorated with Jayhawks. There are even Jayhawks carved into the headboards of the beds and on the outside of the building. Fine arts professor Marjorie Whitney was responsible for the artwork that graced the walls of the sunroom and for the design of the stone carvings on the building's facade. According to the booklet about the hospital, the use of sunflowers and the Jayhawk are special features of the sunroom: "On one panel all Jayhawks are feeling badly, indicating that the location must be unhealthy. Then they discover if they fly up over a door and into another panel, they all get well and feel happy."

Professor Marjorie Whitney painting the wall of the sunroom with sunflowers and Jayhawks.

The completed sunroom.

Jayhawks were carved into the headboards of the student beds in the infirmary.

When the new hospital opened in 1974, the mural was carefully removed from its original location. Thankfully, it was painted on canvas and so could be restored and relocated intact to the second floor of the Watkins Memorial Health Center.

Middle: The center and right side of the Watkins Hospital mural. The sick and injured Jayhawks fly to the right side of the mural when they are well again.

Bottom left: Sick and injured Jayhawks.

Bottom right: A determined Jayhawk pulls a stretcher carrying a sick Jayhawk.

In 1935, Mary E. Standing created a quilt for her brother, John R. Standing, to commemorate his graduation from KU. Although she was only sixteen at the time, the quilt is amazing for its creativity and quality of sewing. The quilt measures seventy-one by ninety-four inches

and has the university seal at its center ringed by Jayhawks. In addition, fourteen Jayhawks, crafted in the style of the 1922 Jayhawk by O'Brien and Hollingbery, are arranged around the quilt. The Jayhawks are delightfully dressed in a variety of costumes that represent various student activities, including basketball and football, entomology (John was an entomology and botany major), and graduation.

Top right: The university seal ringed by Jayhawks.

Middle left: A Jayhawk playing basketball.

Middle right: A Jayhawk playing football.

Bottom left: An entomologist Jayhawk.

Bottom right: A Jayhawk graduate.

The Reserve Officers' Training Corps (ROTC) became established at KU after World War I with the US Army branch of the service. With the increase in US military operations in the 1910s, there were not enough academies or institutes in the country to train officers, so colleges and universities were enlisted to fill the gap. A brochure from the late 1930s described the purpose of the ROTC as "to train and develop men of superior intelligence, sound judgment, ability in leadership, and devoted loyalty to our Democratic Ideals."

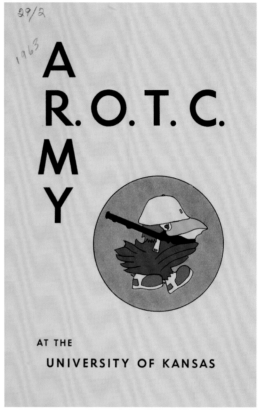

Top left: Army ROTC Military Ball program, April 8, 1938.

Top right: By 1963, the Army ROTC Jayhawk emblem had been updated to resemble the 1946 Jayhawk on this guide to their program.

Left: In 2006, the Jayhawk Battalion of the Army ROTC used this Jayhawk emblem.

During the first part of the twentieth century, the ROTC presence on campus was an on-again, off-again affair. Finally, in 1946, the Army ROTC was reestablished at KU and has been a presence ever since under the name the Jayhawk Battalion. The Navy Reserve Training Corps (NROTC) was started soon after, and in 1947 the Air Force ROTC (AFROTC) was established. The NROTC published a newsletter called the *NROTC Sea Hawk* with their sailor Jayhawk mascot. Guides to their programs informed prospective students about what to expect, and newsletters shared information with students.

Right: The April 1968 issue of the *NROTC Sea Hawk*.

Bottom left: The guidebook to the AFROTC with a Jayhawk that resembled a jet plane on its cover, circa 1950.

Bottom right: Patch used currently by the Air Force ROTC.

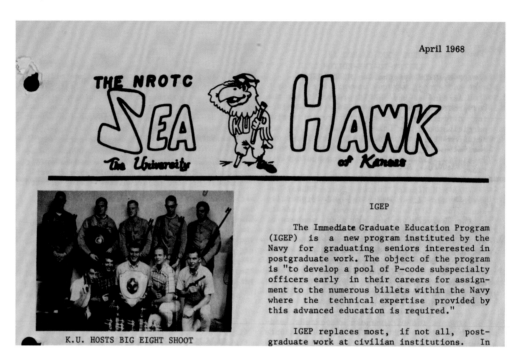

IGEP

The Immediate Graduate Education Program (IGEP) is a new program instituted by the Navy for graduating seniors interested in postgraduate work. The object of the program is "to develop a pool of P-code subspecialty officers early in their careers for assignment to the numerous billets within the Navy where the technical expertise provided by this advanced education is required."

IGEP replaces most, if not all, postgraduate work at civilian institutions. In

K.U. HOSTS BIG EIGHT SHOOT

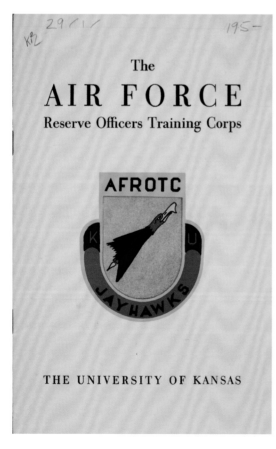

The
AIR FORCE
Reserve Officers Training Corps

THE UNIVERSITY OF KANSAS

The Independent Student Association (ISA) was launched in 1944 as a "new organization, dedicated to the purpose of making the independent student a vibrant part of the University." Independent students did not live in fraternities and sororities and so did not have an instant "family" at KU. The group published a small booklet about the myriad of activities available to students on campus. The ISA also sponsored dances, card parties, picnics, and "fun galore" for independents. Appearing on the cover and on several pages of the booklet is the image of two students marching with the Jayhawk. Because the United States was still involved in World War II, a patriotic theme illustrated the guidebook.

In 1945, the Jayhawk Flying Club was established with an enrollment of sixteen students. To launch the new program, the Ong Aircraft Corporation, a local Lawrence company, sponsored a contest to select an official emblem for the club. Chancellor Malott was one of the judges for the contest. The winning entry, drawn by Jeanne Gorbutt, a member of the club, is a fighting Jayhawk with wings extended for safe and happy flying.

Above: Drawing of the Jayhawk and students from the booklet *The Independents*, 1944.

Left: Chancellor Malott (*center*) and committee judging entries for the contest to choose the emblem for the Jayhawk Flying Club, March 1945.

Above, left: The winning entry from the contest used in an advertisement for the Jayhawk Flying Club in the *Graduate Magazine*, September 1945.

In 1949, Patrick Henry "Pat" Bowers, KU track star and fine arts senior, designed and painted six Jayhawks on the walls of the new west reading room in Watson Library. The murals represented the schools of Journalism, Medicine, Engineering, Pharmacy, Business, and Fine Arts. Unfortunately, the murals lasted for only four years. They were painted over when the Kansas Collection, a library department, needed more space and moved into the area that had served as the west reading room. A student, Bob Worcester, was not happy about the change. He wrote in a *University Daily Kansan* article dated February 12, 1954, that the Jayhawker murals "are now covered by dull green and nauseous brown." He went on to say that the room had been a "showcase of the campus for Jayhawk spirit" but was now just another academic room that was typified by "dull colors and people."

Left: Pat Bowers pointing out his work to another student, *UDK*, January 16, 1950.

Bottom left: The Engineering Jayhawker mural.

Bottom right: The School of Medicine Jayhawker mural.

The Jayhawk was often used to represent students in pamphlets and handbooks. A smiling Jayhawk nurse appears on the cover of the student handbook for the Department of Nursing. The exact date of the handbook is unknown but is probably around 1950. And don't let that cute little Jayhawk nurse fool you. The student nurses were governed by strict guidelines. Included in the booklet is the constitution of the Student Nurses' Association and the association's standing committees. The duties of the House Regulation Committee, in particular, sound quite severe: "to enforce house regulations laid down by the Association, recognize infringements, pass judgment, and mete out punishment for misdemeanors." A proctor was chosen for each floor of the dormitory to "report misdemeanors from her floor" to the committee. One of the more strict rules was a five-minute limit on all telephone calls from the one phone available in the dorm. There were also rules pertaining to the correct way to dress, when student nurses could leave the dormitory, and when they had to be back. The building was locked by ten o'clock on weeknights and 10:30 on weekends.

The Jayhawk was often used to unify students and introduce them to the KU campus experience. One example is a handbook published in the early 1960s titled "Wise Words for Women." Published under the auspices of the Associated Women Students (AWS), it was approved by the dean of women as the official guide for female students. This forty-page booklet was distributed to all female students at KU and addressed new students in particular. Karen Kemp was the art editor for the handbook, which included ten drawings of female Jayhawks. The Jayhawks are drawn as a new Jayhawker at KU, a studious coed, an "active collegian," a well-dressed coed, a socialite, a student seeking information, a "Scholarship Hall or Dorm Dweller," a member of AWS, a worker in AWS, and an obedient Jayhawker who abides by the AWS regulations. These regulations included general conduct, awareness of closing hours, and other rules for dormitories, sororities, and scholarship halls, plus rules governing campus serenading. Also included are directions on where to go to cash a check, change a course, get a Coke, and other useful information.

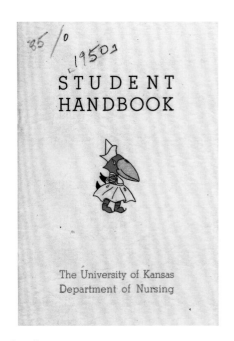

"Student Handbook" for the Department of Nursing, circa 1950.

... As a Student

A studious female Jayhawk.

Where to Go

A female student Jayhawk needing directions.

The Bird and *Disorientation* may have been short-lived student publications, but both were published long enough to create wild and crazy Jayhawks for their covers. Published in 1964, *The Bird* was designed in a satirical fashion as a "higher-planed vehicle of communication" that commented on the "problems and paradoxes—morals, religion, social trends, political issues" confronting its readers. The Jayhawk on its cover looks rather frantic as it tries to tackle these "problems and paradoxes." *Disorientation*, a liberal student publication funded by the KU Student Senate, stated on the cover that it had been "taken over by Anarchists and other scum." This magazine, published in spring 1988, was the "sixties nostalgia" issue.

Above: Cover of the 1964 issue of *The Bird*.

Right: Cover of *Disorientation*, spring 1988.

In 1973, the *University Daily Kansan* ran an ad introducing KU on Wheels, the new campus bus system. The ad featured the new Jayhawk emblem, plus nine other Jayhawks, some of which represented other organizations.

In September 1990, the KU Student Alumni Association hosted a conference for other college and university student alumni associations around the United States and crafted a pin-back button as a souvenir for participants. On the button is the face of a Jayhawk with an oversize beak and glasses with the words "Mount Oread."

Above: 1973 advertisement from the *University Daily Kansan.*

Left: Pin-back button made for the Student Alumni Association conference held at KU in September 1990.

Over the years, the KU Libraries have also used the Jayhawk to catch the attention of students. For example, the KU Libraries enlisted the Jayhawk to advertise its Hawk Help services, to promote reading through a poster campaign, and to introduce the libraries to students.

HawkHelp notification for phone, email, and chat.

Big Jay and Baby Jay show off materials from the University Archives "The Official Sponsor of Tradition" in Spencer Research Library, *Kansas Alumni*, number 5, 2013.

Propelling the Jayhawk into the twenty-first century is the TechHawk used by KU Information Technology (KU IT). In 2013, KU IT was the client for a journalism class titled Strategic Campaigns. The class was divided into teams tasked with preparing proposals to strengthen the information technology brand and improve communications with students, faculty, and staff. Chris Reynolds, creative director for the group that also included Whitney Antwine, Ann Cofer, Cali Forbes, Kelli Klecan, and Hailey Lapin, proposed the concept of a Jayhawk composed of letters and symbols. They named the Jayhawk icon the "TechHawk" and included it in their marketing proposal. KU IT adopted the TechHawk, and Ryan Stueve, the graphic designer, refined the original concept to make it more symmetrical. KU IT has been using the TechHawk in various ways ever since.

New students are welcomed to the University of Kansas with an introduction to KU's traditions, which include the Rock Chalk yell and the Jayhawk mascot. Creating a class banner to be carried at commencement is also a KU tradition, and many classes have incorporated the Jayhawk into their designs. As a result, students are welcomed by a Jayhawk when they first arrive at KU, and a Jayhawk often sends them off when they say goodbye at commencement. Early banners were little more than a flag or pennant with the year sewed onto it. The first class to use the Jayhawk on their banner was the class of 1933. If you look closely, you will see that it matches the Jayhawk from the 1933 *Jayhawker* yearbook. Many other banners have also included distinctive Jayhawks.

The TechHawk used by KU Information Technology (KU IT).

Class of 1936.

Class of 1933 (with those interesting shoes).

Right: Class of 1937.

Bottom left: Class of 1967.

Bottom right: Class of 1969.

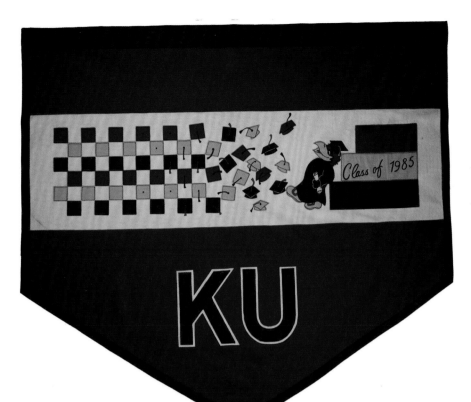

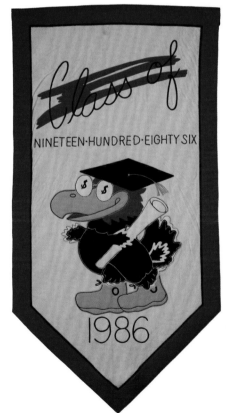

Left: Class of 1985.

Bottom left: Class of 1986.

Bottom right: Class of 2007.

Throughout the decades at the university, the Jayhawk and KU students have been firm friends. Sharing experiences, from the trepidations of beginning life as first-year KU students to victories and losses at sport games, the Jayhawk carries them through to the triumph of graduation.

6 Jayhawks in Advertising

The Jayhawk has been a successful advertising strategy for generations. Throughout the twentieth century, Jayhawks appeared in advertisements for many types of businesses, including clothing stores, jewelers, restaurants, dry cleaners, and hotels, to appeal to the lucrative KU student market. In addition, local businesses began including the word "Jayhawk" in their company names. There was a Jayhawk Café, a Jayhawk Driving Range, Jayhawk Electronics, and the Jayhawk's Barber Shop. It's impossible to drive through Lawrence without encountering a Jayhawk on a storefront or a restaurant wall.

The Lawrence Paper Company has used the Jayhawk as their logo for more than one hundred years. In 1882, KU graduate W. Irving Hill built the first paper mill west of the Mississippi. Sometime between 1901 and 1905, the company began using the brand name of Jayhawk for the part of their company that produced corrugated boxes. The design of the Jayhawk in their ads changed three times over the years. The first was registered as their trademark, the second looks like the Maloy Jayhawk of 1912, and the third is a very industrialized version.

In the 1940s, because their boxes were used to ship materials overseas during World War II, they touted that they were "proudly carrying the name of the Jayhawk to every corner of the world!"

Left: The three different Jayhawk emblems from their company anniversary booklet.

Right: This ad appeared in the September 21, 1946, Texas Christian University vs. KU souvenir football program.

123

The Lawrence Paper Company still uses their Jayhawk image in their factory, on boxes and other products, and for all the world to see on the sides of their trucks in brilliant crimson and blue. To celebrate their centennial, the Lawrence Paper Company created a commemorative medallion with an early Jayhawk and their current version.

Commemorative medallion with two versions of the Jayhawk.

Lawrence Paper Company holiday Jayhawk.

Lawrence Paper Company logo on their truck trailer.

As early as the mid-1910s, a prominent local clothier, Ober's Head-to-Foot Out-fitters, ran many ads in KU football programs, the yearbook, and other publications. In these early ads, they appropriated Jayhawks found in KU publications, such as Maloy's Jayhawk and the crow-like Jayhawk from the 1915 *Jayhawker* yearbook. Eventually, they drew their own Jayhawks for their advertising campaigns. Jayhawks were included in their ads through the business's closure in the 1970s.

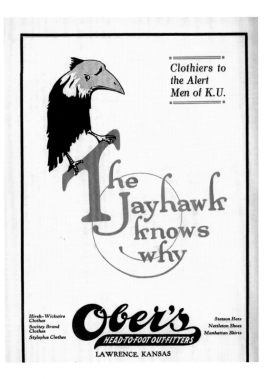

Left: Ober's didn't bother including their whole name on this Jayhawk spirit tag, circa 1915.

Right: Ober's advertisement published in the program for an October football game in 1915. This Jayhawk appears in several different publications including the *Jayhawker* yearbook of 1915.

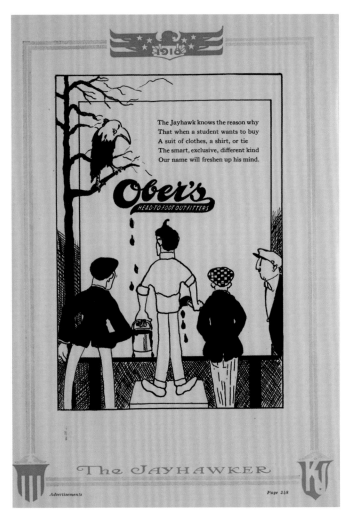

Left: This interesting ad for Ober's ran in the 1918 *Jayhawker*, 348.

Above: This Ober's ad with two very interesting Jayhawks appeared in the November 29, 1923, football program, 14.

Right: Jayhawk Jacks were issued by Ober's Boys Shop and could be exchanged for "valuable prizes" circa 1960.

Middle: Advertisement from the September 26, 1935, football program, 1.

Bottom left: Rowlands "Booksellers to Jayhawkers" published this ad in the 1915 *Jayhawker* yearbook, 422.

Bottom right: The winning Rowlands Book Store ad from the 1930 *Jayhawker* submitted by Jane Kirk.

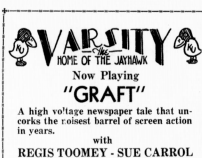

VARSITY
the HOME OF THE JAYHAWK

Now Playing
"GRAFT"
A high voltage newspaper tale that un-
corks the noisest barrel of screen action
in years.
with
REGIS TOOMEY - SUE CARROL

Starts Monday
For 3 Days
DOUG FAIRBANKS, JR.
As a ravishing, lovable, rascal in the
kind of role you've always wanted him
to play—
"I LIKE YOUR NERVE"
with
LORRETTA YOUNG
A Happy, Breezy Story of a Boy in Love

Other businesses across Lawrence also included Jayhawks in their names or advertisements for years. The Varsity Theater, one of three theaters on Massachusetts Street, called themselves the "Home of the Jayhawk" and included in their ads images that resembled the 1922 Jayhawk.

Rowlands College Bookstore, established in 1898 and located near campus, used a very studious Jayhawk for their advertisement in the 1915 *Jayhawker.* They changed their advertising every few years, each time incorporating new Jayhawks. Rowlands even held an annual contest for students to draw Jayhawks for their ads.

ROWLANDS
Booksellers to Jayhawkers
KANSAS

"Where Students Go"
+++
The
K U
Store
+++
Rowlands
College Book
Store
14th & Ohio Streets
Lawrence : Kansas

AT THE EDGE OF
THE CAMPUS

KU
1898   1930

Wise Jayhawkers
go the ROWLANDS way

---gifts
---books
---stationery

Booksellers to Jayhawkers
Rowlands
COLLEGE BOOK STORES
14th and Ohio   1237 Oread

This is the winning ad in our annual
ad contest won by Jane Kirk 1930.

In 1955, the Rowlands building was converted to a restaurant called the Wagon Wheel Cafe. This family-style restaurant was not successful, but the situation soon turned around once they began serving beer. The iconic bar became a major student hangout known more often as "the Wheel." Now Jayhawks are incorporated into the Wheel's logo, and Jayhawks decorate the walls inside.

Left: The Wheel's welcome sign with their official logo.

Below: An example of one of the Jayhawk paintings on the wall of the Wheel.

During the 1920s, the Jayhawk Cafe used Jayhawks named Ray and Harry (the names of the owners) to lure students to their restaurant by placing ads in the *K-Book* and the *Daily Kansan*. The Jayhawk Cafe still exists in the same location at 1340 Ohio—just around the corner from the Wheel.

Above: The outside of the Jayhawk Cafe, 1991.

Left: *University Daily Kansan*, September 13, 1922.

In 1929, the Hotel Jayhawk in Topeka lost a lawsuit filed by Jim O'Bryon and George Hollingbery. The artists of the 1922 Jayhawk had already copyrighted their version of the bird, and they believed that the Jayhawk in the hotel ads too closely resembled their Jayhawk. The lawsuit must not have had much of an effect, because even after they lost, the hotel continued to use a Jayhawk similar to the 1922 version. The Hotel Jayhawk opened in 1926 with their iconic neon Jayhawk on full display on top of the building. During the 1950s, the hotel regularly ran ads in the *Kansas Alumni* magazine, such as their September 1953 advertisement that touted their location as the "Off-The-Campus Headquarters for 'Barbs' and 'Greeks' since way-back-when." At the time, they were also operating the Jayhawk Junior Hiway Hotel.

Advertisement published in the *Kansas Alumni* magazine in September 1952. Note that they had also opened the Jayhawk Junior Hiway Hotel.

128

Let the Other birds
go South for the winter
I'll stay in the warm

HOTEL JAYHAWK

in Topeka

Kansas Alumni magazine, 1954.

The iconic neon Jayhawk still glows as a city landmark atop the Jayhawk Tower building in downtown Topeka, Kansas.

Also of note is the Jayhawk Theatre, which was adjacent to the hotel. This luxurious venue opened in 1926, could seat fifteen hundred, and was fully air-conditioned, which made it a trendsetter of its day and very popular through hot Kansas summers. It was placed on the National Register of Historic Places in 1974 but soon closed in 1976. The building now operates as Jayhawk Towers, with offices and event spaces, and the theater hosts special events.

This neon sign from the outside of the building is now on display in the renovated Jayhawk Tower.

Some recognized Jayhawk artists drew their Jayhawks for local companies. In an ad that appeared in many different publications during the 1960s, Independent Laundry and Dry Cleaners used both Paul Coker's Lawrence High School Chesty Lion mascot and Coker's Jayhawk in their advertisements. The laundry used a whole flock of Jayhawks in the imaginative ad they ran in the 1963 *Jayhawker*. The laundry at Ninth and Mississippi only recently closed and now houses a restaurant.

Even though the Jayhawk in this ad for the Granada Theater is not attributed, it has some of the characteristics of the Paul Coker Jayhawk with the very large beak.

Independent Laundry & Dry Cleaners ad from the 1960 *Jayhawker*.

This advertisement for the Granada Theater was published in the 1952 *K-Book*.

Independent Laundry and Dry Cleaners ad from the 1963 *Jayhawker*, 106.

The Jayhawk on the window of Owens Flower Shop is well known because of its proximity to KU's campus and location on a major street. There has actually been a Jayhawk at that location for nearly fifty years. James V. Owens purchased the shop from the original owners of University Floral in 2009. In the late 1970s, the original owners had adopted the 1912 Jayhawk holding a bunch of mixed flowers as part of their logo. After Owens acquired the shop, he slightly redesigned the Jayhawk to have him hold a bouquet of red roses instead of mixed flowers.

Jayhawk on the window of the Owens Flower Shop, 2022.   Owens Flower Shop sign, 2022.

Even major national companies such as Dairy Queen and the Campbell Soup Company have incorporated Jayhawks into their local ads, particularly those supporting KU sports.

Dairy Queen as a local supporter of KU sports in 1984. Image from the basketball program for December 1, 1984, 12.

131

Campbell's® Salutes **KU** Basketball!

A Campbell Soup advertisement from 1987 "Salutes KU Basketball."

Right: Santa Fe Trailways advertisement from the 1937 *Jayhawker.*

Facing page: "Whatever the heck 'Rock Chalk Jayhawk' actually means" ad from 1995.

Jayhawkers Go Santa Fe Trailways

Valued patrons of Santa Fe Trailways are the men and women of Old K.U., who have long since learned that bus travel is quick, convenient and economical. Serving every important city and town in Kansas, sleek, cream-and-crimson Trailways Streamliners have carried thousands of Jayhawkers back home for the holidays, week-ends, summer vacations. This fine patronage of K.U. people has helped build Santa Fe Trailways — a Kansas institution in its beginnings — into a far-flung transportation organization, now serving many another state.

For all of which our thanks and appreciation. And to the Class of 1937 — the best of luck, health and happiness.

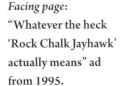

SANTA FE TRAILWAYS

General Offices — Wichita, Kansas

The Santa Fe Trailways bus company took a Jayhawk along for the ride, and Target created a very clever advertisement that appeared in KU basketball programs in 1995.

Use of the Jayhawk image and the name "Jayhawk" is now closely protected by the university. As the university's brand web page expressed in 2021, "Our symbols unite us. The Jayhawk, the crimson and blue, and the KU signature all express KU pride and tradition. The brand itself is intangible, an idea in the minds of our community and our audience."

The term "Jayhawks" became a federally registered

Whatever the heck "Rock Chalk Jayhawk™" actually means,
we mean to be here shouting it every game this season.
Good luck KU, from your loyal fans and proud alumni at Target.

service mark in December 1978, and in January 1979 the drawing of the 1946 Jayhawk was also approved as a registered trademark. At that time, the Kansas Union bookstore managed the university's trademarks. In an August 1981 interview with the *Lawrence Journal-World* newspaper, Steve Word, the general manager of the bookstore, noted that the registered Trojan warrior logo for the University of Southern California brought in well over $1,000,000 a year. He said that the Jayhawk "may be a source of revenue for the university" but was doubtful about the fighting bird's chances of ever making as much money as USC's fighting Trojan: "KU's name is not known worldwide, so it will never be that big. It is just a way some revenue can be brought in for its usage." In the same article, Vicki Thomas, KU general counsel, said the primary reason for registering the bird was to give the university control over its use. "The university didn't file the service mark primarily because we were interested in collecting royalties, but because we were interested in protecting its use," Thomas said. All royalties the university receives from Jayhawk licensing go toward student scholarships and student programming initiatives.

The Office of Trademark Licensing is now under the purview of Athletics. In 1988, when Kansas won the National Basketball Championship, licensing became even more important. There was a proliferation of use of university brands, particularly the Jayhawk on T-shirts, including some that were controversial and that resulted in a lawsuit filed by KU.

In addition to the word "Jayhawk" and the design of the final Jayhawk, other examples of university brands include the university seal, and the phrases "Rock Chalk Jayhawk," and "The Crimson and the Blue." Any product bearing an identifiable mark that can be interpreted as representing the University of Kansas must be licensed.

The success of KU's licensing program is the subject of an article published in the January 1996 issue of *Off Campus Retailer* magazine, titled "The Program Underdog No More, Jayhawks Chalk Up National Attention with Athletic Success." The author of the piece, Thomas Bullington, states, "Having a good mascot is vital to achieving success at retail for universities, and this is one part of the equation Kansas has had figured out for some time." The official Jayhawk mascot and character logo have stood the test of time.

7 Jayhawks for Sale: Memorabilia, Collectibles, Souvenirs, Merchandise

For more than a century, Jayhawks have been re-created in many forms. They have been molded into lamps, clocks, and statues made of clay, bronze, glass, plaster, and wood. They have been printed on ties, hats, scarves, and even cowboy boots. They have been painted on walls and signs, carved into headboards and onto the stone blocks of buildings, baked into cookies, and molded into butter for fancy KU events.

The first person to mold the bird into a statue was Milton Nigg, an engineering student who modeled Hank Maloy's Jayhawk into a statuette in 1914. Made from plaster, the five-and-three-quarter-inch statue bore the words "Prosperity" on the front of its base, "Jayhawk" on the left side, and "Kansas" on the right. Stamped on the back is Nigg's mark "©1914MWNIGG Lawrence Kansas." The Jayhawk sold for forty cents and could be purchased at four different bookstores, according to an ad that appeared in the second issue of volume two of the *Sour Owl*.

Bottom left: Advertisement for the Nigg Jayhawk, in *Sour Owl* 2, no. 2 (June 1915).

Bottom right: This particular Nigg Jayhawk was purchased by Gertrude Jensen "in the bookstore" in 1914. Which bookstore is unknown.

Pennants were popular items students used to decorate their dorm rooms to show school spirit. One pennant in particular displayed a great-looking football player Jayhawk. The age of this pennant is not known, but KU football players wore leather helmets like the one depicted on the Jayhawk's head during the 1920s.

KU football pennant, circa 1920s.

Since that first Jayhawk statuette was sold in 1914, thousands of objects have borne or been molded in the likeness of the Jayhawk. The University Bookstore in the Student Union is the primary purveyor of all things Jayhawk.

Just outside the bookstore on the second floor of the Student Union is a truly amazing display of Jayhawk items, originally collected by local businessman Kenneth "Bud" Jennings. Jennings had acquired Jayhawk memorabilia for more than sixty years and amassed more than one thousand pieces. In 2010, when Jennings began thinking about selling the collection to help with his retirement, he struck an agreement with the Student Union, allowing them to display parts of his collection. Jennings was hopeful that someone who saw what he had amassed would be interested in purchasing the collection as a whole so it would not be broken up. But after four years and no offers, Jennings asked for the collection to be sent back to him. Mike Reid, coordinator of KU history for the Student Union, was in the process of boxing up all the pieces when he learned that KU alum James Ascher and his wife, Mary Ellen, of Shawnee Mission, were interested in purchasing the collection in its entirety and donating it all to the university. They had learned about the Jennings Jayhawks through the local media and did not want the collection to be broken up.

The Aschers donated $130,000 for the purchase of the Jennings collection and also contributed to new exhibit cases built specifically to display the collection to its best advantage. The Ascher Family Collection had its grand opening with a ribbon-cutting ceremony on January 29, 2015.

Facing page: **Cases holding a portion of the Asher Family Collection.**

Facing page: Case
commemorating
George Knotts and
his Jayhawks. The
large stone Jayhawk
is at the center of the
case.

These four clay
figurines of Jayhawks
in a variety of poses
are probably from the
1950s.

Also of note is the artist featured in the endcap case of the exhibit area, Jayhawk artist George Knotts. His story is much like that of other Jayhawk artists before him. Knotts was a 1955 fine arts major who, at the request of Chancellor Franklin D. Murphy, made the first known stone Jayhawk. It is now on display on the second floor of the Student Union.

While Knotts was still a student, the University Bookstore requested that he sculpt a small bronze Jayhawk to be sold as a paperweight. Over the years, that Jayhawk has been attached to pedestals and given as gifts to particular groups, such as members of the Gold Medal Club, namely alumni who are celebrating the fifty-year anniversary of their graduation. One unique feature of this Jayhawk is that Knotts designed it to look like it is smiling on one side and frowning on the other. After retiring as a graphic designer, he would sometimes set up in the Student Union on football game days and create his artwork for football fans. Knotts also illustrated a Jayhawk coloring book that was published by the KU Memorial Union.

Above, left and right: Both sides of a Knotts bronze Jayhawk. This one was presented to the Gold Medal Club of 1984. Turn it one way and it's smiling; turn it the other way and it's menacing.

"Color-Me-Jayhawk" coloring book illustrated by George "Hawk" Knotts.

140

8 JAYHAWKS NEAR AND FAR

In 2009, the University Archives received an email from the administrative assistant to the dean of the School of Journalism, asking if the archives would be willing to house a hand-carved Jayhawk that had been discovered in Flint Hall. The statue was described as being about five or six inches high and mounted on a wood base but was unfortunately broken into two pieces. Written in pencil on the base were the words "Sent to L. N. Flint, alumni Secretary by Conrad Hoffman, YMCA at a German internment Camp in 1917."

The University Archives replied that it would be happy to welcome the Jayhawk statue into its collections. Accompanying the Jayhawk was a photocopy of an article from the October 23, 1921, *Kansas City Star* titled "The Bolshevik Jayhawk." Obviously this little statue had a history. The author of the story reported that the editor of the *University Daily Kansan* had recently received a package containing "a carved wooden image of the Kansas Jayhawk" and that statue had been found by a KU student, Conrad Hoffman, in a German prison camp.

The true story had been published in the *UDK* on September 28, 1921, under the title "Jayhawk War Captive, Back to Native Land." Conrad Hoffman did indeed spend time in Germany, but rather than being a KU student, he was secretary of the university's YMCA and had gone to Germany as a YMCA worker to provide aid to prisoners in war camps.

UDK article from September 28, 1921, regarding the prison camp Jayhawk.

In the article, it was reported that L. N. Flint, secretary of the Alumni Association, had received a small wooden statue in the mail that looked very much like a Jayhawk. No note accompanied the statue to identify the sender. Several days later, a letter from Conrad Hoffman, the secretary of the KU Young Men's Christian Association (KUYMCA) arrived. Hoffman explained to Mr. Flint that he had found the wooden Jayhawk in a prison camp in Germany and that its origin was unknown. The article also reported that the bird would "be mounted and placed in the Journalism Museum." A photograph of the museum taken during that time period does indeed show the little Jayhawk statue in the lower center of the large display case in the center of the room. A photograph of the statue was also included in the 1922 *Jayhawker*.

Jawhawk War Captive, Back to Native Land

Two days ago Professor Flint received a package containing a little Jayhawk carved from wood. There was no note or identification tag of any sort attached to the little bird, so that Professor Flint was in ignorance as to the why and wherefore of its arrival.

This morning, however, there came a letter from "Con" Hoffman, former Y. M. C. A. secretary here, who was last on the hill the year of '19 and '20, explaining to Mr. Flint that he had found the wooden Jayhawk in a priso ncamp in Germany. The bird's origin is unknown. It will be mounted and placed in the Journalism Museum.

Above: Journalism Museum, circa 1920s.

Right: Close-up of the Jayhawk statue in the case.

So back to 2009—the pieces of the statue were carefully placed in a box containing other university artifacts until it was brought out to show to a *UDK* reporter who was writing a story about unusual items that could be found in the University Archives. This article caught the attention of Marc Greenberg, chair of the Department of Slavic Languages and Literatures. Professor Greenberg visited the archives to see the statue and was immediately taken with its story. With assistance from Dr. Greenberg's department and Spencer Research Library, the statue was cleaned and repaired by a conservator. It was displayed in the department for one year and then returned to the University Archives. Professor Greenberg continued his research into the history of Conrad Hoffman and his statue, and in 2010 his article "Hoffman's Hawk: A University of Kansas Jayhawk Carved during the Russian Revolution of 1917 Reappears at KU in the Twenty-First Century" was published in KU ScholarWorks, the digital repository of the University of Kansas.[1]

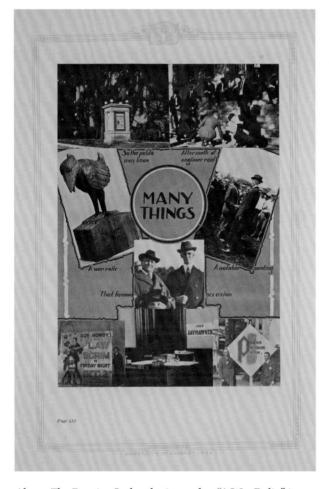

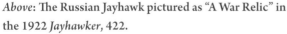

Above: The Russian Jayhawk pictured as "A War Relic" in the 1922 *Jayhawker*, 422.

Right: The Russian Jayhawk safely laid to rest in a specially designed box in the University Archives.

As has been noted in other chapters, military groups often adopted the Jayhawk as a mascot or symbol, incorporating the word "Jayhawk" into their name or using the Rock Chalk chant as their battle cry. After the end of World War I, the Kansas National Guard was stationed in Sampigny, France. While there, the soldiers published the *Jayhawker in France* as the unofficial organ of the 137th Infantry Regiment (First Kansas) of the Kansas Army National Guard. Only a few issues made it into print, the first on January 29, 1919.

In September 1923, a story appeared in the *University Daily Kansan* announcing that five thousand cardboard Jayhawk gliders were being printed for a football trip to West Point. The plan was that the four-inch folded bird would be sailed in every town of importance between

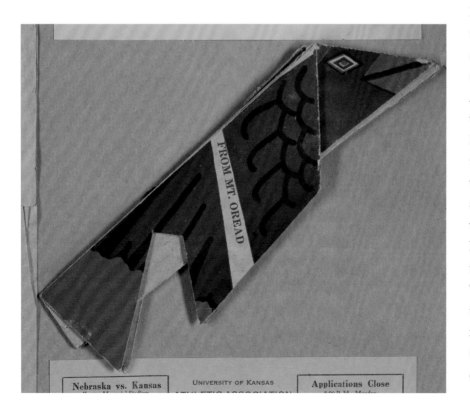

Lawrence and West Point and that there would be messages about KU and Lawrence printed on it. The idea was presented to Athletics Director F. C. Allen, who gave his approval. "Before I definitely decided to accept the bird," Dr. Allen said, "I went to the top of the stadium and shot him into space. It was worth a 'million dollars' to see him soar, and I at once knew that the idea would be a success." The only extant example of the Jayhawk glider has been found in the scrapbook of Bob Gilbert, who was a yell leader during his time at KU.

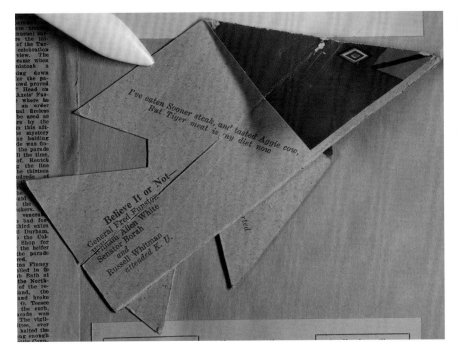

Robert Gilbert scrapbook, 1919–1923, 137. The message inside proclaims, "I've eaten Sooner steak, and tasted Aggie cow, But Tiger meat is my diet now!"

The photograph of the back of an airplane pilot was published in the May–June 1942 issue of the *Graduate Magazine*. On the back of the pilot's flight jacket can be seen the large patch of a Jayhawk riding a bomb. The owner of the jacket was KU graduate Robert Raymond, a Royal Air Force (RAF) pilot, who had joined the war in England before the United States entered World War II. Known as "Kansas" to his fellow pilots, Robert had written home to his mother asking her to have a Jayhawk patch made and sent to him. He wanted a patch with a Jayhawk in the right colors standing on a bomb with the RAF symbol on it. The patch measures roughly thirteen inches by eight inches.

By a strange twist of fate, that very same patch is now in the Kansas Collection at the Spencer Research Library. The patch and Raymond's diary are part of a collection of letters and other memorabilia donated by the Raymond family.

Jayhawk In R.A.F.

Fellow fliers in the Royal Air Force call Robert F. Raymond, b'34, "Kansas." Not at all ashamed of the title, he got his mother in Kansas City to have a Jayhawk emblem made and sent to him last fall. Now on his back as he guides bombers over Germany rides the Jayhawk, as shown above. Bob is a sergeant pilot.

Patch from the Raymond Family Papers, Kansas Collection.

"Jayhawk In R.A.F" piece from the *Graduate Magazine*, May–June 1942.

Several KU graduates had images of Jayhawks painted on the sides of their planes during World War II. In 1998, Harold E. Goss sent a photograph and letter to the director of the Alumni Association. The photo showed Goss as a pilot sitting in his P-47 Thunderbolt, with a Jayhawk painted on the engine cover. He explained that he had taken a KU calendar when he went overseas in 1944 and had asked a crewman if he could paint the Jayhawk in the calendar on the side of his plane. Goss said that he wanted a fierce Jayhawk with a five-hundred-pound bomb under his wing.

Another World War II pilot, Lt. Col. Jay B. Smith, is pictured standing in front of his B-26 Marauder bomber with the 1929 Jayhawk on the side. That Jayhawk is also holding a bomb under its wing. The photograph was taken on June 24, 1944.

Below: Harold E. Goss in his P-47D Thunderbolt with the 1941 Jayhawk painted on the engine cover, 1944.

Right: World War II pilot, Jay B. Smith, and his B-26 Marauder with his Mr. Jayhawk mascot.

The JAYHAWK VII CORPS 48th Anniversary 1918 ✶ ✶ ✶ ✶ 1966

Forty-eighth anniversary publication of the Jayhawk VII Corps.

Another military group that adopted the Jayhawk long ago is the Civil War–era VII Army Corps that dates to 1864, when the Corps was placed under the command of Maj. Gen. Frederick Steele. Stationed in Arkansas, two-thirds of the division were Kansas troops bringing with them the appellation "Jayhawkers."

From Peru to Mexico City, Jayhawks can be found in strange places. In July 1954, professor of geology Walter Youngquist, while visiting the ancient city of Chan Chan in Peru, noticed birdlike figures carved into rock. Thinking that these carvings resembled Jayhawks, he wrote in his notes: "Evidence now comes from South America to indicate that the Jayhawk survived on that continent until at least the time of the Inca Empire."

Photograph taken by Walter Youngquist of a carving he discovered on a wall in the ancient city of Chan Chan.

In the University Archives is a mysterious photograph of the Banco Nacional de Mexico in Mexico City taken in 1960. The words "Restaurant" and "KU" can clearly be seen with what looks like a Jayhawk in the center. The origin of this photo is unknown. Why would there be a Jayhawk Restaurant in Mexico City?

Photograph of the KU Restaurant on the Banco Nacional de Mexico building in Mexico City, 1960.

The Western Jayhawk Motel located in St. George, Utah, was owned by Jack and Jackie Werts, both KU alumni. The photo was taken in 1975.

A stuffed Jayhawk on the set of *Today* with Jane Pauley and Tom Brokaw.

In 1978, on the *Today* show, host Tom Brokaw read a story that had appeared on national wire services about KU economics professor Malcolm Burns. Burns, who described himself as "cheap," usually gave a lecture on the last day of class on the art of being cheap and having fun while doing it. He described using coupons and refund offers and switching bank accounts to receive gifts, including blankets, cookware, a stuffed Jayhawk, and more. At that point in the story, Brokaw paused and wondered aloud on the air, "What is a stuffed Jayhawk?"

He soon found out. Over the next week, the NBC office received several Jayhawks in the mail sent by alumni from around the country. Taken by the response, Brokaw brought one of the Jayhawks on the show the following week. The story and photo appeared in the "Along the Jayhawk Walk" section of the *Kansas Alumni* magazine for April 1978.

The prize for the most "far out" Jayhawk can be given to KU grad and astronaut Steven Hawley, who flew during the ninety-fifth launch of the Space Shuttle in July 1999 and carried a KU T-shirt.

Photograph of astronaut Steven Hawley taken in July 1999 while on the ninety-fifth launch of the Space Shuttle.

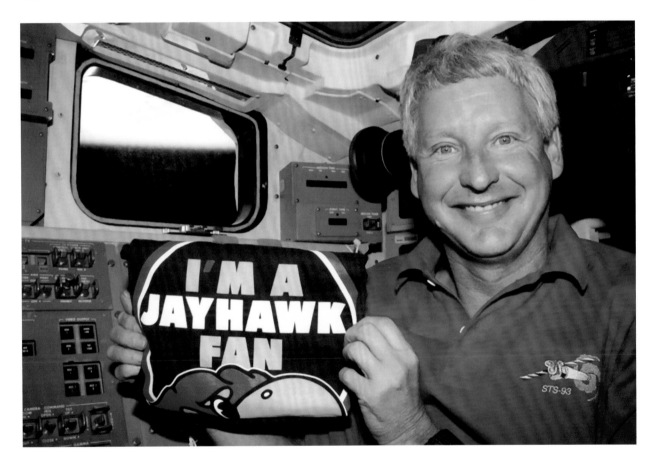

In 2002, a project called Jayhawks on Parade was hatched that would propel the Jayhawk into tourist attraction status. The idea originated with the board members of the Lawrence Convention and Visitors Bureau after members had seen or heard of cities that sponsored whimsical animal parades, such as parades of colorful cows, dolphins, or Easter Bunnies on the Country Club Plaza in Kansas City, Missouri.

The purpose of the project was threefold: to bring visitors to Lawrence to view the statues, to boost community morale, and to benefit nonprofit organizations. Each bird had an identified location and a sponsor who chose the artist. The thirty decorated Jayhawks were on display around the city from April through November 2003. After that, each individual organization chose whether to auction their Jayhawk off or to keep it.

Some of the Jayhawk names and locations were Mardi Gras on the Kaw Hawk at the Lied Center of Kansas, John Brown Hawk at the Lawrence Journal-World News Center, and Uncle Sam Hawk at the Lawrence Service Center on I-70.

Years later, several attempts were made to locate all the Jayhawks. Some were found in their original locations or inside a nearby building, some were now at private residences, and a few had simply disappeared. A few still exist in high-profile places, such as the Merhawk on the Kaw outside McLain's Market at 1420 Crescent Road and the Classic Jayhawk in front of the Kansas Union. The Classic Jayhawk is actually a replica, as the original was damaged by vandals, and it does have regular touch-ups because children love to climb on it.

"Lions and Tigers and Hawks. Oh My!" Jayhawk at the Hilltop Child Development Center.

Notes

1. Accessed October 25, 2022: https://kuscholarworks.ku.edu/bitstream/handle/1808/6896/Russian_Jayhawk_history_2010Nov24_MLGreenberg.pdf.

9 Jayhawks into the Twenty-First Century

For anyone who doubts the continued strength of Jayhawk creativity among KU students, there are multiple recent examples to ease their mind. On March 29, 2017, Hannah Coleman wrote a piece for the *UDK* announcing that KU had updated the Hawk Route, "a little-known perk of the University" that makes up a "stairless path designed to help students with physical disabilities navigate the campus with ease." For this update, Catherine Johnson, the director of the ADA Resources Center for Equity and Accessibility, asked design students to help create a new logo for the route. Design student Piper Holt is responsible for this new Jayhawk, cleverly incorporating in the logo a KU building that we see every day.

Jayhawk GPS (Guidance. Persistence. Success.) is the brainchild of Academic Success. The system is designed for use by all undergraduate advising units as they assist students to schedule appointments, review their appointment notes, see upcoming campus deadlines, and more. The imaginative symbol of a Jayhawk face shaped like a map pin was created by Leah Nicholson and has been in use since 2018.

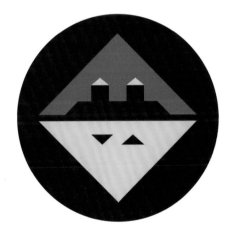 

Left: Hawk Route icon created by Piper Holt.

Right: Symbol of the Jayhawk GPS program.

A major Jayhawk event occurred on March 7, 2019, with the ribbon cutting of the new Ascher Plaza and unveiling of six large bronze Jayhawks that had been installed in the plaza area on the south side of the Student Union. Reconstruction on Jayhawk Boulevard provided an opportunity to improve the large empty space. The renovations led the Student Union to include six large pedestals to the plaza in anticipation of the installation of a set of the evolution of the Jayhawk statues.

The Student Union began reaching out to possible donors, and James Ascher Sr. again stepped up and agreed to donate $200,000 to the project. Additional money came from Phi Gamma Delta, class of 1980. The search then began for a sculptor to create the statues. Happily, there was a KU alum just waiting to do that very thing. Matt Palmer and his uncle Robin Richerson, who sculpted the statues, had dreamed for years of having Jayhawks as giant monuments on campus.

The first five Jayhawks in the bronze evolution stand three feet tall and weigh between one and two hundred pounds. The 1946 Jayhawk is larger, standing five feet tall and weighing more than six hundred pounds. The impressive statues ring the plaza, providing a wonderful space for people to gather for photographs at graduation and other events, and are among the first things visitors see as they enter campus at the Student Union entrance.

Right: The 1912 Jayhawk on the Ascher Plaza.

Below: The 1946 Jayhawk on the Ascher Plaza.

Joining the Jayhawk display in the Union plaza is another group of Jayhawks in bronze. Named the "Jayhawk Nest Monument," the large statue was unveiled on September 23, 2022, as part of KU's annual Family Weekend celebration. The artists Robin Richerson and Matt Palmer provided a description:

> The Jayhawk Nest Monument was cast in bronze and weighs 905 lbs. The nest itself has a diameter of approximately 60 inches (or 5 feet) and a variable height of 12″ to 14″. A 3-foot cast bronze "Mother Jayhawk" is perched at guard on the perimeter of the nest as her Baby Jayhawks are in various stages of hatching from their eggs. One 18-inch "Baby Jayhawk" is fully hatched and stands opposite the Mother on the edge of the nest. The egg shell for the fully hatched "Baby Jayhawk" has already been discarded by the mother to help protect the baby birds from predators. Another cast bronze "Baby Jayhawk" with a height of 18″ is standing within an open/hatched egg shell that is down inside of the nest. And, to help honor the 100th Anniversary of the "1923 Jayhawk" edition, the monument also features an egg within the nest in the early stage of hatching . . . with the beak/head of the "1923 Jayhawk" breaking through the shell of the egg.

The Jayhawk Nest Monument unveiled on September 23, 2022.

During the spring of 2020, the University of Kansas campus was closed along with every college and university campus across the country due to the worldwide COVID-19 pandemic. As the university struggled to keep things as normal as possible, groups began meeting via Zoom video conferencing. On April 2, 2020, the chancellor and key members of the administrative staff reached out to students, faculty, and staff to share messages of hope and reassurance. The words "Jayhawk" and "Jayhawks" were used many times in an effort to remind us that we were a community and would confront this (hopefully) once-in-a-lifetime, shared experience together.

The Jayhawk was a key participant in the effort to eliminate COVID-19 from KU's campuses. Keeping six feet apart was one of the cautionary measures people were urged to adopt, and the huge image of the Jayhawk on a banner with arms outstretched was a visual reminder to students and everyone who visited the KU campus to obey that rule. The wearing of masks was another cautionary measure that the Jayhawk adopted. In these and other activities of the university, the Jayhawk was an active member.

Above: "This Is 6 Feet" banner used in the Protect KU Together campaign.

Right: Big Jay in a mask at a KU basketball game.

Watkins Health Services have also enlisted the Jayhawk in their COVID safety messages, using the same happy beak image as for their Be*ak* Healthy logo.

When classes resume every fall, students are welcomed back with much fanfare. Freshmen especially receive special attention, with many events planned to introduce them to life at KU. Hawk Week and Unionfest are longtime traditions. Unionfest, organized by Student Union Activities (SUA), introduces students to the many services offered by the Student Union. The poster for the 2022 event, created by student designer Julia Gillman, includes a particularly colorful, dynamic Jayhawk demonstrating that Jayhawk creativity lives on in the 2020s.

"BEak Healthy!" elevator door in the Watkins Memorial Health Center, 2022.

Unionfest poster for 2022.

Hawk Week design
for 2021.

Every year, the week before classes start in the fall, Hawk Week engages students arriving on campus in a full week of activities. For Hawk Week 2021, Summer Foster, senior art director in KU Marketing, designed a Jayhawk based on the Academic Jay statue in front of Strong Hall to convey many messages to students. On the Jayhawk, words invoked KU's values, such as involvement, traditions, and connections. The Jayhawk decorated T-shirts and posters put up all around campus. Fun events for luring students to engage in campus activities included music performances, open houses, tours, a scavenger hunt, and Fossil Friday.

Every year, visitors to KU are given a guide that invites them to take a walking tour of campus that highlights specific buildings, gathering spaces, and natural places such as Potter Lake and Prairie Acre. Included in the invitation is the opportunity to wander Mount Oread and encounter "Jayhawks across Campus": "Whether cast in bronze, painted in wild technicolor, or beaming from behind a display case, there's no shortage of one-of-a-kind *objayhawks d'art* to find across campus. Don't worry, your bird-watching tour won't require binoculars—just this handy guide and a comfortable pair of walking shoes (preferably oversized and yellow)."[1]

In the most recent addition to the KU experience, the new Jayhawk Welcome Center, the mascot is front and center. Visitors can explore all that KU has to offer and customize their Jayhawk journey by using QR code scanners at six different interactive zones. Included are "The Jayhawk Experience," featuring immersive videos that showcase KU traditions; "The Jayhawk Network," where guests choose from a list of alumni success stories; and finally, the "Origins and Traditions" exhibit, which features both video and display cases on the history of the Jayhawk and the Rock Chalk chant with appropriate artifacts.

* * *

The Jayhawk remains an important part of life at the University of Kansas and, owing to the university's close relationship to the community at large, in the city of Lawrence as well. For more than a hundred years, students have used their boundless imaginations to create Jayhawks that are truly unique, despite the hundreds drawn before them. Whether it's an athletic event, a student group or activity, KU publications, or city businesses, Jayhawks seem always to find their way into the action. Trying to imagine the University of Kansas or indeed the city of Lawrence without the Jayhawk is difficult to do—almost as difficult as separating the heart from the body. Perhaps that is a bit dramatic, but KU certainly includes the Jayhawk in almost everything it does. There will always be someone to take up the challenge of creating a new Jayhawk to be added to the mascot's more than one-hundred-year history. The university continues to fully embrace its mascot and symbol, thus keeping the Jayhawk tradition alive and strong.

Notes
1. University of Kansas, Office of Marketing Communications, 2021–2022 Visitors Guide, 40.

Index

Page numbers in **bold** refer to photographs.

Academic Jay, 35, 83; statue, **36**, 156
Academic Success, 151
ADA Resources Center for Equity and Accessibility, 151
"Adventures of the Bull Dog on The Gridiron" (Maloy), 45
Air Force ROTC (AFROTC), 112; guidebook of, **112**; patch, **112**
Allen, Forrest C. "Phog," 26, 29, 144
Allen Fieldhouse, 13
"Along the Jayhawk Walk" (*Kansas Alumni*), 149
Antwerp Olympics, 9
Antwine, Whitney, 119
Army ROTC, 112; emblem, **111**; military ball program, **111**
Ascher, James, Sr., 136, 151
Ascher, Mary Ellen, 136
Ascher Family Collection, 136, 138; cases holding, **137**
Ascher Plaza, 151; Jayhawk on, **152**
Associated Women Students (AWS), 115
Athletics Department, 24

B-26 Marauder, **146**
Baby Jay, 40, **52**, **53**, **54**, **55**, **57**, **58**, **59**, **60**, **118**, 153; basketball and, **57**; as Batman, **61**; Big Jay and, **58**, **59**; birth of, 52–53, 55–59, 62; body of, **52**; egg of, **53**; as Elvis, **62**; first birthday of, **55**; in holiday sweater, **61**; physical demands of playing, 56; rescue of, **57**; in tuxedo, **59**; at wedding reception, 58, **58**
Bailey, E. H. S.: Jayhawk yell and, 5, 44
Banco Nacional de Mexico, 147, **147**
banners, 119, **119**, **120**, **121**

"Basketball at the . . . University of Kansas" (booklet), 7
basketball Jayhawk, **68**, **110**
basketball uniforms, 26, **27**, 59, **60**
Baughman, Robert: cartoon by, 107
beak glasses, **102**
Beak Healthy, 85; elevator door, **155**; logo, 155; newsletter, **85**
Beta Theta Pi house, **99**
Bibler, Richard Neal "Dick," 105; drawing by, 82, **82**; Jayhawk of, 36–37, **37**; yearbook page of, **37**
Big Blue Eggventure, The (Downs and Orth), 90, **90**
Big Jay, **22**, 50, **51**, **54**, **92**, **118**, **154**; Baby Jay and, 53, 57, 58, 59; as Elvis; **62**; in holiday sweater, **61**; physical demands playing, 56; as Robin, **61**; in tuxedo, **59**; at wedding reception, 58, **58**
Bilotta, Mrs. Vince, 50
Bilotta, Vince, 50
Bird, The, 116, **116**
Bitter Bird, 36, 37
Blackmar, Frank Wilson, 11, 13
Blair, Streeter: scrapbook of, **16**
Blake Hall, **63**
"Bolshevik Jayhawk, The" (*Kansas City Star*), 141
bonfire, **96**, **98**
Booth Family Hall of Athletics, 50
Bowers, Patrick Henry "Pat," 114, **114**
Bowles, George H. "Dumpy," 24
Bradley, Everett L., 9
Brokaw, Tom, **148**, 149
Brown, Ed, 34
Bryan, William Jennings, 21; cartoon of, **20**
Budig, Gene: greeting card of, **41**
bulldogs, 44, **44**, 45, 46, **46**
Bullington, Thomas, 134

Burk Awning & Canvas Goods Manufacturing Co., 56
Burkhart, Eileen: scrapbook of, **93**
Burns, Malcolm, 149

Campbell Soup, advertisement by, 131, **132**
"Campus Chirps Back" question, **86**
Canfield, Arthur G., 4
Cardoza, Lela Duncan: scrapbook of, 107
Carlos, Don, 15, **16**
Carter Tire and Supply Company, 26
Centennial commemorative medallion, 39, **39**
Centennial Hawk, 40, **40**
Chalmers, Laurence: Baby Jay and, 53, **54**
Chan Chan, Peru, 147, **147**
cheerleaders, 24, **29**, 48, **48**, 107
Chesty Lion, 39, 130, **130**
Cicala, 63
Civil War, 1, 2
class banners: Class of 1933, **119**; Class of 1936, **119**; Class of 1937, **120**; Class of 1967, **120**; Class of 1969, **120**; Class of 1985, **121**; Class of 1986, **121**; Class of 2007, **121**
Classic Jayhawk, 150
Cleveland Plain Dealer, 26
Coca-Cola, 34
"Coed Jayhawker," **83**
Cofer, Ann, 119
Coker, Paul Allan, Jr., 105; illustration by, **105**; Jayhawk of, 36–37, **38**, 39, 130; yearbook page of, **38**
Colcord Park, Oklahoma City, 46
Coleman, Hannah, 151
Collegiate Manufacturing Company, 48
"Colonel Funston leading his dashing Kansans, their thrilling war-cry 'Rock Chalk, Jay Hawk! K.V.!,'" **10**

"Color-Me-Jayhawk" coloring book
(Knotts), **140**
Colton, John B., 1
Cornhusker, image from, **47**
Country Club Plaza: parade on, 149
COVID-19, 85, 153, 155
"Crimson and the Blue, The," 105, 134

Dairy Queen: advertisement by, 131, **131**
Denver University, 81
Department of Geology, 84
Department of Nursing, 115; handbook
for, **115**
Devlin, Patrick, 1, 28, 79
Dineen, Patrick, 80
Disorientation, 116, **116**
Doc Jayhawk, 32; bronze statue of, **33**
Downs, Deeann, 90
Dyche Hall of Natural History, 11, **11**

Edwards, Betsy Hollingberry, 26
El Dorado Times, 32
Emporia Gazette, 2
English, Roger, 35
entomologist Jayhawk, **110**
Eureka Democratic Messenger, 21

Faculty Man, 18, **20**, 21
Fambrough, Don, 88; book by, **88**
Families of Freedom Scholarship Fund,
32
Family Weekend celebration, 153
"Fanciful Foolishness for Football Fans"
(Minturn), 106
Fighting Jayhawk, 37
Firemanship Training Program: annual
report of, 84, **84**
Flint, L. N., 141
Flint Hall, **141**
Folgers Coffee, 34
football Jayhawk, **68**, 88, **110**
football programs, **16**, 24, 76, **76**, 77,
77, 78, **78**, 124; advertisement from,
123, **125**, **126**
football uniforms, 59, **60**
Forbes, Cali, 119
"For the Defense of the Nation" (*Gradu-
ate Magazine*), **81**
Fossil Friday, 157
Foster, Summer: Hawk Week and, 157
Frazee, Joseph Robaldo, 11

Free University, 72
French, Laura M., 2
Fritz Tire Company, 26, 31; Jayhawk
applique by, **30**
Frosh Hawks, 107, **107**; patch for, **107**
Frosty the Snowman, 39
Funston, Frederick, 9

Geology-Hawker (G-Hawker), 84, **84**
George P. Hollingbery Corporation, 26
G-Hawk, 84
Gilbert, Bob, 144
Gillman, Julia, 155
Gold Medal Club, 138; Jayhawk of, **140**
Gorbutt, Jeanne, 113
Goss, Harold E., 146, **146**
Graduate Magazine, 13, 23, **23**, **27**, 28,
30, 31, 63, 75, 78, 78, 80, **80**, **81**, 82,
82, 145; homecoming and, 96; Maloy
and, 78; opening page of, **75**, **76**
Granada Theater, advertisement by, **130**
Green, Kelly, 85
Greenberg, Marc, 143
greeting cards, **41**
grotesques, **11**, **12**
Gustafson jewelry store, 26

Hamilton, Tracee, 56
"Happily Ever After" (O'Bryon), 26
Happy Jayhawk, 34, **34**, 40, **40**
Harlan, Byron G., 18
Hawk hats, **103**
Hawk Help, 118, **118**
Hawkins, Lauren, 13
Hawk Route, 151; icon for, **151**
Hawk Week, 155, 156; design for, **156**
Hawley, Steven, 149, **149**
Hearst Papers, 26
"Heathcliff," 31, **32**
Helianthus, 7, **8**, 63
"Heoweez," 31, **32**
Hill, Aeo: scrapbook of, **93**, **94**
Hill, W. Irving, 123
Hilltop Child Development Center, **150**
Historic Kansas City Foundation, 34
History of the Jayhawk, The (Hollingberry
and O'Bryon): illustration from, **25**
History of the State of Kansas (Jennison),
2
Hoch Auditorium, 67
Hoffman, Conrad, 141, 143

"Hoffman's Hawk," (Greenberg), 143
holiday cards, 41, **41**
holiday Jayhawk, **124**
Hollingbery, George Phillips, 24, **25**,
34, 48, 128; Hearst Papers and, 26;
Jayhawk and, 26, 77
Holt, Piper: icon by, 151, **151**
homecoming, 96, **98**, 99, **99**, 100, **100**,
101
Home Economics Department, 83
Hotel Jayhawk, 26, 128, 129; advertise-
ment for, **128**, **129**
"How and When 'Rock Chalk' Came
into Being" (Bailey), 5, **6**
"How Did the Jayhawk Get This Way?"
(Shore), **27**, 28
Humble, Emma, 2; book by, **3**
Hurst, Amy, 52, 53, **54**, **55**, 57
Hurst, Richard, 53
"Huskers Produce Stolen Jayhawk"
(*UDK*), 47

"I'm a Jayhawk" (Bowles), 24; sheet
music for, **24**
Independent, The: drawing from, **113**
"Independent Kansas Jay-Hawkers"
poster, **2**
Independent Laundry & Dry Cleaners,
130; advertisement by, **130**
Independent Student Association
(ISA), 113
Iowa State Cyclones, **81**

"Jaybirds Plan to Share Nest" (press
release), 58
Jayhawk, **15**, **43**, 48, **49**; anthropomorphic qualities of, **103**; chorus line,
40; costume for, **46**, 49, **49**, **50**;
emblems, **29**, **111**, 113, 123, **123**;
evolution of, 28, 41, **41**; figurines,
138; first cartoon of, 18, **18**; first
official, 64–65; headboard, **109**; in
military uniform, 81; running track
and, 68; signature, 34–35; singing
and, 68; statue, 33, 36, 142, 156;
sticker, **40**; term, 4, 15, 43, 154;
web-footed, 82
Jayhawk (1912), 40, **40**, **41**, 42, **152**; described, 17–22, **22**; floor inlay of, 39
Jayhawk (1920), 42; advertising with,
23; described, 23–24

Jayhawk (1922): described, 24, **25**, 26, 28; variants of, **27**

Jayhawk (1923), **42**, 153, **153**; floor inlay of, **39**

Jayhawk (1929), **42**; described, 28–29, **29**, 31

Jayhawk (1941), **31**, **42**; described, 31–32

Jayhawk (1946), **152**; described, 34–35, **34**

Jayhawk Audubon Society, meeting notice for, **84**

Jayhawk Battalion of the Army ROTC, 111, 112; emblem, **111**

Jayhawk Book, The (Humble), 2, **3**

Jayhawk Cafe, 123, 128, **128**; advertisement for, **128**

"Jayhawk Chalk Talks" (*Graduate Magazine*), 75, **75**

Jayhawk Cleaners, 26

Jayhawk Club of Kansas City, 28, 29; emblem of, **29**

Jayhawk Driving Range, 123

Jayhawk Electronics, 123

"Jayhawker commando," **104**, 105

Jayhawker in France, The, 144, **144**

Jayhawker M.D., 32, 33, **33**

Jayhawkers, 37, 48, 146; appearance of, 49; described, 2; term, 1, 43

Jayhawker yearbook, 5, 8, 15, 18, 31, 36, 37, **44**, 45, 63, 64–65, **65**, **66**, **67**, 70, **70**, 71, **71**, 72, **72**, 73, **74**, 75, 77, 91, 96, 104, 119, 124, 125, 126, 130, 141; advertisement from, **130**; cartoons in, 67; illustrations from, 69, **69**, 72, **72**, **73**, **74**; image from, **15**; pages from, **4**, **6**, **32**, **45**, **48**, **63**, **65–69**, **91**, **103**, **143**

Jayhawk Flying Club, 113; advertisement for, **113**; emblem, **113**

"Jayhawk for President," 100, **101**

Jayhawk gliders, 144, **144**, **145**

Jayhawk GPS, 151, **151**

Jayhawk Gridster, 77, 77, 78, **78**

Jayhawk hats, **102**

"Jayhawk in R.A.F." (*Graduate Magazine*), **145**

Jayhawk Jacks, **126**

JayHawk Journalist, 41, 83, **83**

Jayhawk Junior Highway Hotel, 128; advertisement by, **128**

Jayhawk Nation, 57–58

Jayhawk Nest Monument, 153, **153**

Jayhawk paintings, **127**

Jayhawk Posters (company), 26

Jayhawk Quill, The, 64, **64**

"Jayhawk Rebellion," 100, **100**

Jayhawk Restaurant, 147, **147**

Jayhawk's Barber Shop, 123

Jayhawks on Parade, 149–150

Jayhawk sun visors, 102, **102**

"Jayhawk Talks," 64, **65**

Jayhawk Theatre, 129

Jayhawk Tower, 129, **129**

Jayhawk II, 49

Jayhawk Walk: illustration of, **89**

"Jayhawk Walk" (Podrebarac), **89**

Jayhawk Welcome Center, 157

Jay Janes, 107, **107**

"Jazz Showdown" (Podrebarac), **89**

Jennings, Kenneth "Bud," 136

Jennison, Charles R., 2; carte de visite of, **2**

Jensen, Gertrude, 135

Jinx, 18, **18**, **19**, **20**, 21, **93**

Joe College, 104, **104**

John Brown Hawk, 150

Johnson, Catherine, 151

Jolly Jayhawk, 2

Journalism Museum, 141, **142**

Kansas Alumni, 18, 22, **22**, 26, 37, 39, 50, 56, 63, 75, 85, 88, 128, 149; advertisement from, **128**; illustration from, **88**, **89**; photo from, **58**, **59**

Kansas Army National Guard, 144

Kansas Business Magazine, 13

Kansas City Art Institute, 34

Kansas City Journal: cartoon from, **16**

Kansas City Star, 141

Kansas City Times, 17, 28, 29; illustration from, **29**

Kansas Collection, 114, 145

Kansas Day, 2

Kansas Historical Quarterly, 82

Kansas National Guard, 144

Kansas Relays program, **76**, 85, **85**

Kansas State Agricultural College, 17–18, 46, 67

Kansas State Historical Society, 79, 80

Kansas State Teachers College, Emporia, 2

Kansas State University, 17–18, 57

Kansas Union, 134, 150; renovation of, 39

Kansas Volunteers, 9

Kaw Hawk, 150

K-Book, The, 105, **105**, 128; illustration from, **104**

Kemp, Karen, 115

Kenneth Spencer Research Library, 57, **118**, 143, 145

Klecan, Kelli, 119

Knotts, George "Hawk," 138; case commemorating, **139**; coloring book by, **140**; Jayhawk of, **140**

Krishtalka, Leonard, 11

KU Alumni Association, 13, 26, 28, 29, 32, 37, 40, 48, 49, 50, 52, 56, 63, 75, 80, 88, 146; brochure by, 35, **35**; Jayhawk and, 23, 24, 34, 41; Jayhawk Nation and, 57–58

KU Biodiversity Institute & Natural History Museum, 11

KU Club, 24

KU Directory and Yellow Pages, **40**

KU Information Technology (KU IT), 119; TechHawk of, **119**

KU Libraries, 118

KU Marketing, 156

KU Medical Alumni Association, Doctor/Nurse Jayhawks and, 32

KU on Wheels: advertisement for, 117, **117**

KU Press Club, 107, **107**

KU Restaurant, **147**

KU ScholarWorks, 143

KU Student Alumni Association, 117

KU Student Senate, 116

Lapin, Hailey, 119

Lawrence Convention and Visitors Bureau, 149

Lawrence High School: mascot of, 39, 130

Lawrence Journal-World, 134

Lawrence Journal-World News Center, 150

Lawrence Outlook, 21; cartoon from, **22**

Lawrence Paper Company, 123, 124; advertisement by, **123**; holiday Jayhawk of, **124**; truck trailer of, **124**

Lawrence Police Department, 56

Lawrence Service Center, 150

Lazzarino, Chris, 85

Leslie's Weekly: drawing from, **10**

Liberty Bowl: Big Jay/Baby Jay at, 59, **62**
Lied Center of Kansas, 150
Life at Laurel Town in Anglo-Saxon Kansas (Stephens), 23
Lindley Hall, 84
"Lions and Tigers and Hawks. Oh My!" Jayhawk, **150**
"Little Man on Campus" (Bibler), 37
Los Angeles Times, 26
Lusk, C. W., 15
Lyon, Maclay, Jr., 28, 29

Madden, Pauline, 15; scrapbook of, **16**
MAD magazine, 39
Malott, Chancellor, 113, **113**
Maloy, Daniel Henry "Hank," **17**, 18, 21, **21**, **22**, 28, 39, 40, 46, 50, 93, 96, 100; cartoon by, **18**, **19**, **20**, **22**, **47**, **79**; Jayhawk of, 17, 35, 45, 62, 64–65, 123, 124, 135; letter from, 78–79; scrapbook of, 21
Manly, William Lewis, 1
Marshall, Mary Olive: cartoon by, **104**
Maytag, 34
McGuire, Mickey, 29
McIntyre, Emery: scrapbook of, **93**
McLain's Market, 150
Mechem, Kirke: booklet by, 79, 80, **80**
Memorial Stadium, 56
Memorial Union, 40, **55**, 138
Mercury (Roman god), 69, **69**
Merhawk on the Kaw, 150
"Mickey Jayhawk" stickers, 29
Minturn, Benjamin, 106; illustration by, **106**
Missouri Tiger, 50, **50**, **93**, **97**, **99**, **100**, 105, 106, **106**, 107; attacking, 67, **67**
Moore, Raymond C., 31; essay by, **30**; G-Hawk and, 84
Morozzo, Dede, 58
Mother Jayhawk, 153
Mr. Jayhawk, 64, **146**
Murphy, Beulah: scrapbook of, **44**, **93**
Murphy, Franklin D., 138
Musser, Noah: Weather Jay by, 85, **86**
Mythical Jayhawk, The (Mechem), 79, **80**

Naismith, James, 15
National Basketball Championship, 50, 134
National Invitational Tournament, 50

Natural History Museum, 11, 31
Navy Reserve Officer Training Corps (NROTC): newsletter by, 112, **112**
Nicholson, Leah, 151
Niethammer, Deborah Hollingbery, 26
Nigg, Milton, 135
Nigg Jayhawk statuette: advertisement for, 135, **135**
NROTC Sea Hawk, 112, **112**
Nurse Jayhawk, 32; illustration of, **115**

Ober's Boys Shop: Jayhawk Jacks from, **126**
Ober's Head-to-Foot Out-fitters, 28, 124; advertisement for, **28**, **125**
O'Bryon, James "Jimmy" Edward, 24, **25**, 48, 128; Jayhawk and, 26, 77
Off Campus Retailer, 134
Office of the Chancellor, 41
Office of Trademark and Licensing, 134
Olympics, Antwerp, 9
"Once a Jayhawk, Always a Jayhawk," 100, **101**
137th Infantry Regiment (First Kansas), 144
Ong Aircraft Corporation, 113
Oread, 8; page from, **9**, 63
"Origins and Traditions" exhibit, 157
Orth, Jennifer Embrey, 90
"Our Yells" (*Oread*), **9**
Owens, James V., 131
Owens Flower Shop, 131; window, **131**; sign, **131**

P-47D Thunderbolt, 146, **146**
Palenshus, Dave, 58, **58**
Palmer, Matt, 152, 153
Pauley, Jane, **148**
Pearson, Larry Leroy, 88; illustration by, **88**
pennants, 45, 136, **136**
pep clubs, 107, **107**
Phi Gamma Delta, 151
Pioneer Pete (Denver University), **81**
Podrebarac, Charlie: illustrations by, 89, **89**
postcard, **93**
Postlethwaite, Carl A. "Posty," 107
Powers, Mary Helen (Harper): scrapbook of, **95**
Prentice, Syd: illustration by, **63**

prison camp Jayhawk, 141
Protect KU Together campaign, 154
Pruett, Eldon, **54**

Quenstedt, Theresa, 53

Radcliffe Chautauqua Company, 21
Raymond, Robert, 145, **145**
Raymond Family Papers: patch from, **145**
Red Peppers, 107
Reid, Mike, 136
Reserve Officers' Training Corps (ROTC), 111, 112
Reynolds, Chris, 119
Richerson, Robin, 152, 153
Ritland, John C., 72
"Rock Chalk, Jayhawk K. V.," 9
"Rock Chalk, Jay Hawk" yell, 4, 5, 9, 13, 15, 44, 105, 119, 132, 144; as university brand, 134
Rock Chalk: term, 7
Roosevelt, Theodore, 9
ROTC (Reserve Officers' Training Corps), 111, 112
Rowlands Booksellers to Jayhawkers: advertisement by, **126**
Rowlands Book Store: advertisement by, **126**
Royal Air Force (RAF), 145
Royals Stadium, **51**
Rudolph's Shiny New Year, 39
Russian Jayhawk, **143**

Sandy, Harold David "Hal," 34, 40; Jayhawk of, 34, **34**, 35, 40
Santa Claus Is Comin' to Town, 39
Santa Fe Trailways: advertisement by, 13, 132, **132**
Sauer, George, 80
Scannell, Daniel, 42
Scannell Jayhawk: 1912, **42**; 1920, **42**; 1922, **41**; 1923, **42**; 1929, **42**; 1941, **42**
School of Journalism, 83, 114
School of Medicine Jayhawk, **114**
School of Social Welfare, 108
Schultz, Paul, **57**
"Science, Psychology & Rock Chalk" (*Helianthus*), 7, **8**
Science Club, 57

scrapbooks, 15, **16**, 21, **92**, **93**, **94**, **95**; keeping, 92

Senior Night, **59**

VII Army Corps, 146; publication of, **146**

Seventh Kansas, 2

Seventy-First Infantry Division, 31

Shore, Chester K.: article by, **27**, 28

Sixty-Eighth Annual Commencement, invitation to, 83

Smith, Jay B., 146, **146**

Snodgrass, Laddi, 56

Snow, Francis, 7

Sokoloff, David: Jayhawk by, 85

Sour Owl, 31, 36, 105, **106**, 107; advertisement from, **135**; cartoon from, 106, **106**

Space Shuttle, 149, **149**

Squire, Con, 17

Steele, Frederick, 146

Stephens, Kate: book by, 23, **23**

Stevens, Cathy, 56

Strauss, Richard, 53

Strong Hall, **36**, 49

Student Nurses' Association, 115

Students' Handbook, 105

Student Statewide Activities Association: brochure by, 35, **35**

Student Union, 136, 138, 151, 152, 155

Student Union Activities (SUA), 155

Summer Olympics (1920), 9

sun visors, **102**

Target: advertisement by, 132, **133**

TechHawk, 119, **119**

Tefft, C. E., 49

Tefft, Eldon, 35, 49

"They Gotta Quit Kickin' My Dog Aroun" (song), 18

Third US Army, 31

"This Is 6 Feet" banner, **154**

Thomas, Vicki, 134

Thorpe, Merle, 17

Three Little Jayhawks, The (Fambrough), 88, **88**, 90

"Tight Wads" (cartoon), 64, **64**

Tinsdale, Katharine, 26

Today show, **148**, 149

Trueman-Gardner, Katherine, 90

Twente Hall, 108

2001: A Space Odyssey, 53

UDK. See University Daily Kansan

Uncle Sam Hawk, 150

Unionfest, 155; poster for, **155**

Union plaza, 153

University Archives, 22, 32, 46, 57, 118, 141, 143, 147

University Bookstore, 34, 134, 136, 138

University Calendar, 31, **31**, **32**

University Courier, 5

University Daily Kansan (UDK), 13, 17, 18, 21, 31, 36, 46, 47, 52, 56, 64, 85, 114, 117, 128, 141, 143, 144, 151; advertisement from, **117**; article from, **141**; cartoon from, **18**, **20**, **47**; on Jayhawk, 48

University Floral, 131

University of Kansas Centennial (1866–1966) medallion, 39, **39**

University of Kansas Endowment Association, 41, 53; logo of, 87, **87**; promotional calendar of, **87**

University of Kansas Extension Service, 84

University of Missouri, 5, 28, 64, 67; game against, 24. *See also* Missouri Tiger

University of Nebraska, 47, 62

University Review, 5

university seal, **110**

USS *Radon (Raton)*, 82

Van Keuren, Catherine: memory book page of, **92**

Veit, Christopher, 59, **59**

Virtue, Jessica, 59, **59**

Wagon Wheel Café, 127, **127**

Walsh, Reggie, 80

Walton, Anthony, 7

Washington Post, 26

Watkins, Elizabeth M., 108

Watkins Health Services, 155

Watkins Memorial Health Center, 85, 109, **155**

Watkins Memorial Hospital, 108, **108**; mural at, **109**

Watson Library, 114

Weather Jay, 85, **86**

Wells Overlook tower, 56, 57

Werts, Jack and Jackie, 148

Western Jayhawk Motel, **148**

"What the Jayhawk Stands For" (Blackmar), 11

White, William Allen, 21

Whitla, Lowell R., 82

Whitney, Marjorie, 108, **108**

Wilkerson, Janet: scrapbook of, **94**

Williams, Gene Varner "Yogi," 31, 32, **32**, 82, 105; illustration by, **105**; Jayhawk by, 31, **31**

Williams, Roger, 84

Williams, Wade L., 32

Willie the Wildcat, **43**, **81**; abuse by, 56–57

Wintermotte, Dick, 49, 52

"Wise Words for Women" (AWS), 115

Worcester, Bob, 114

Word, Steve, 134

Years on Mount Oread, The (Taft), 4

yell leaders, **10**

Young Men's Christian Association/ Young Women's Christian Association, 105, 141

Youngberg, Irvin E., 53

Youngquist, Walter, 147; photo by, **147**